The little Girl in the Window

A True Ghost Story

The Little Girl in the Widow

A True Ghost Story

by

John Anthony Adams

Custom Books Publishing
2008

Dedication

This book is dedicated to Tom Hagman, the most amazing person I have ever met. Tom has been my guide to a mind- boggling exploration of the "other side."

The Author

John Anthony Adams has a Ph.D. in soil science from the University of California at Riverside and worked for years as a scientist with the U.S. Bureau of Land Management. He is the author of four books, including *Dirt,* a popularized science book about soil*, Dangling from the Golden Gate Bridge and Other Narrow Escapes*, a collection of very unusual narrow escapes from death. *Rialto*, a photo history of Rialto, California, and *Ronnie's Nine Lives*, a hilarious true life collection of stories about a very adventurous boy's years of growing up dangerously in the 50s and 60s. John Adams is the historian of the Rialto Historical Society and is working on a book about life in Southern California during the days when orange groves covered much of the land. He owns and operates the last orange grove in Rialto, a town that at one time contained 10,000 acres of groves.

1   A Skeptic in the World of the Spirits

For most of my life I have been convinced that there is no survival after death, and naturally did not believe that there were such things as ghosts and the spirit world. When I was young I believed there was a god, although I am not sure whether it was a Christian god, since I don't recall believing in an afterlife. I grew up in a small town with a number of churches and believing in God was part of life. My god was probably of my own design, combining the beliefs of the town and my family with what I was able to glean from my own experience. I became enraptured with science by the time I was ten or eleven years old and had no doubt that there either was or would be a natural explanation for everything, including an afterlife. If such things as ghosts existed, wouldn't at least some of them be clever enough to provide proof of their existence in such a clear way that even scientists would be convinced of it?

As you might expect, I did not discuss such matters a great deal, because it was socially much easier to profess a mild belief in God and much less risky to avoid any talk of ghosts. Obviously only poorly educated deeply superstitious people would believe in such things as disembodied but yet real spirits. Little did I realize that I was going to be forced to revise my thinking forty years later!

I studied hard in school to become a scientist, and did well. I was a National Merit Scholar, a member of Phi Beta Kappa, and a Magna cum laude graduate of Pomona College, a prestigious liberal arts college in Claremont, California. I earned my bachelor's and master's degree in Botany and was particularly interested in evolution. I completed my Ph.D. in soil science at the University of California at Riverside and then worked for the Department of the Interior as a soil scientist. I authored or co-authored many articles in scientific journals and was well on my way to a philosophy of life that certainly did not include such things as demons and spirit portals (more about such things later.)

Although I did not believe in ghosts, I was perhaps not completely closed-minded, since I had always enjoyed ghost stories. I was thrilled by the chilling movie, "The Innocents," which was made in 1961. It was based on Henry James' famous story, "The Turn of the Screw." It starred Deborah Kerr as an inexperienced 19th century governess who became aware that the two apparently angelic children in her care were under the corrupting influence of evil spirits. The outstanding direction of Jack Clayton, and the fine acting, dark photography, ominous and lonely setting, haunting sound effects and musical score, and brilliant script make it the finest of several filmed versions of Henry James' novel, and one of the most sinister and frightening ghost movies ever made. This movie made me seek out other books and movies about ghosts that gave me a spooky feeling that I for some reason found very enjoyable. Nonetheless, I don't believe that I regarded ghosts as any more real than the subjects of science fiction and other fantasy stories that I also enjoyed. I must admit, though, that I would have felt uneasy at the thought of spending the night by myself in a cemetery, so I must have had some hidden traces of superstition in my subconscious.

A number of years after seeing the movie, I heard a ghost story from my cousin, Skip Sapp, that made me wonder if there really could be something to the idea of ghosts. When I read books about ghosts, I always assumed that the story had been fabricated or was strictly the result of someone's overactive imagination. Hearing Skip's story was different because I knew him to be an extremely reliable observer with an excellent memory. He is a retired Tucson teacher of impeccable character and someone whose observations I totally trust.

In the 1940s Skip, along with his mom, dad, brother, and sister, escaped the fierce summer heat of their Arizona farm by staying in a mountain cabin in Pine Valley, California. Skip had recently returned from Europe where he had served in the army in World War II. His story was that after they had first moved in they noticed an unaccountably cold area in a hallway of the cabin. There was no evidence of a draft that could explain the feeling of chill. The family was also puzzled because their dogs refused to go through the hallway, and stood at the entrance of the hallway and howled.

One night, when everyone was in bed, Skip heard his mother screaming. Skip and his brother and sister ran to their parents' room, and found his mother in a terrible state of fear. She said she had seen a man standing in the hallway outside the open door of the bedroom. Skip's dad had been asleep, was awakened by her screaming, and saw nothing. Skip's mother said the man was tall and was wearing a military uniform. The family rushed all through the house but could not find anyone.

The family was greatly perplexed by this incident. Skip received an even greater shock one day when he was talking to a man he knew who operated a riding stable where people could rent horses. He told the stable operator that his mother had seen a man in a military uniform in the hallway outside her bedroom, but the family couldn't find a trace of him when they searched the house. The man at the stables said, "That was Colonel Springer. He committed suicide in that hallway." He went on to say that the Colonel always wore his uniform, and was tall and very erect.

But until a few years ago my life was generally free of thoughts of ghosts. Neither had I discussed them with other people. My friends would have worried about my mental state if I had. My immediate family consisted of a brother who is a Caltech trained engineer and a mother and father who were more than skeptical about such things. Above all, I never brought up such topics with my distinguished professors. In my recent years, to my great surprise, I told a couple of these professors about my adventures with ghosts and discovered that they also had personal ghost stories to tell.

My ghost adventures began innocently enough because of my activities in a small museum. I live on the only remaining orange grove in an area in Southern California that used to be entirely devoted to the citrus industry. It is an island of green surrounded by a seemingly endless sea of subdivisions, industrial buildings, shopping centers, and general developmental damage. My grandfather planted the grove in 1907, and I love it and everything it stands for. I retired from my job as a soil scientist some years ago and spend my time caring for the orange grove and writing books. I live with my mother who was born on our grove. She was in her 80s during most of the period of time covered in this book.

The first book I wrote was called "Dirt." It was about soils and oriented toward the lay reader. The second was about very unusual narrow escapes from death and was called "Dangling from the Golden Gate Bridge and other Narrow Escapes." Then I decided to write the definitive work on the conversion of Southern California from an area in which citrus played a major role to its present state. The working title of this book is "The Vanishing Orange" and I have been working on it for years. As part of the process I have interviewed hundreds of people whose memories of Southern California extend far back into its rural past. The more I did this, the more I became interested in the history of Rialto, the town in which I live. I then began spending large numbers of hours investigating archival materials that are maintained by the Rialto Historical Society. This led to increasing involvement in this historical society, with the result that I am now its official historian. The headquarters of the historical society is in a gracious and nicely restored old church building in the town, which has been partly converted to serve as a museum. It is also haunted. It was here that my odyssey with ghosts began.

Initially I began to take detailed notes simply as an aid in evaluating the evidence. I didn't expect to accumulate enough material for a book. When it eventually began to look as though I could get enough stories for a short book, my first thought was that I could intersperse the ghost stories from the church with other input about ghosts gleaned from my reading. I had never written a book before about a subject that didn't have an enormous body of widely accepted written information. After I began to read about ghosts, I learned that I could not place a high level of trust in anything that I read. Maybe some or even a lot of it was true but how could I be sure? There were great differences between authors in many of their explanations about ghosts, and theories about the origins, nature, and behavior of ghosts that looked to me like nothing more than wild speculation. Thus I had to start from scratch in my quest to learn about ghosts. The ghosts in the church supplied a bounty of stories and insights, and I met several miraculous people who helped show me the ways of the spirits.

The journey has been marvelous. I have experienced convincing demonstration after convincing demonstration that there are ghosts in the old church. After each my mind would conclude, "This can't be true. There must be a logical explanation for this." A lifetime of skepticism had formed habits of thought that were almost impossible to change, despite powerful evidence to the contrary. It took years of encounters before I could accept that there was something to this ghost thing, but when I did it totally undermined my old belief system. It was thrilling to discover that existence did not end with death. It is also a bit bewildering and scary to discover there is an afterlife because I know so little about it except for the ghost part. I probably never will know any more with certainty until I get there. I can't get the answers from faith, as most religious people do, because I must have evidence before I can believe things. I have also found it maddening that I can't convince all the skeptics I know that ghosts are real.

One reason that many people find it impossible to take ghosts seriously undoubtedly comes from the word "ghost" itself. It is a loaded word that has been associated with ridicule probably for as long as it has been in use. But what is a ghost? It is a soul stuck in the land of the living.

Skeptics say that evidence for ghosts is only anecdotal, and then they put forth an arbitrary rule that such evidence is not reliable. They conclude that ghosts can't be real because they have never been confirmed by any other data. If skeptics were called for jury duty and while being questioned about their opinions expressed a view that use of anecdotal evidence is a totally unacceptable way to search for the truth, they would be the ones thought to be nuts. If ghosts are bunk because they have not been confirmed by scientific data, then so are souls and so is God. The reason most prominent skeptics refer to ghosts as nonsense, but do not describe souls and God in the same way, is their fear of becoming the targets of ferocious outrage. Ghost hunters and other enthusiasts of the paranormal are much safer targets.

Thomas Hobbes, the famous 17th Century English Philosopher, considered the idea of the soul to be contradictory, since it consists of an "immaterial material." I would have agreed before my experiences in the church, but after having observed many extraordinary manifestations of ghostly activity which were also noted by numerous other reliable witnesses, I am certain that the immaterial beings are real. Probably the most unusual feature of this ghost investigation is the extraordinarily large number of observers involved. The close agreement between witnesses was not simply a result of wishful or fearful thinking by one person that spread the same impressions to others by the power of suggestion. Many cases will be discussed in which someone sensed a certain ghost or some particular actions of a ghost without being aware that others had already noticed the same things. This occurred, for example, when I observed spectral activity and then heard someone else state the exact same observation before I had a chance to mention it. It also happened in some cases when people made their first visit to the church without having heard the ghost stories, and they would report the same perceptions that others had noticed earlier.

Are there physical properties associated with a ghost that could be measured? I am not aware of any truly serious attempt by a first-rate scientist to collect data about ghosts. The use of temperature sensors, magnetometers, Geiger counters, or any other such familiar equipment by ghost hunting enthusiasts without scientific training can hardly be expected to provide a definitive answer to the question of what science can learn about ghosts. I wonder what an extremely creative team of scientists might discover if they investigated ghosts with very advanced equipment. Maybe nothing, but who knows? It is very unfortunate that no highly capable researchers appear to take the subject of ghosts seriously.

I first realized that I was a firm believer in the spirit world when my reaction to death changed dramatically. Previously, I was horribly shocked when anyone that I had known or even merely heard or read about had died. It was such a terrible thought that they were gone forever. Then, I started to react differently to reports of people's death, thinking, "They still exist." This book describes part of this journey – the adventures of a skeptic in the land of the spirits. If you believe in such things, may it reinforce those beliefs. If you do not, may it make you wonder.

2   The Haunted Church

The stately old First Christian Church towers high over the decaying, oldest part of the city of Rialto, California, a little over 50 miles east of Los Angeles. It has not been used for worship since 1963, when its minister and congregation left to move to a new church building in another part of the city. The old church's basement and adjacent Sunday school building provide a home for an appealing little museum of the town's vanished past as a small-town farming community. Now, except for a single orange grove that my mother and I own, the agriculture is all gone. The city of Rialto has a population of over 100,000 people of diverse ethnic groups rather than the 2,000 who lived here when it was an orange-growing town. The old church building, which can no longer be used for church services since it is owned by the city, is rented for weddings to raise money for the local historical society.

Around 1992, a group of people began to meet regularly for card games in the basement of the church on Thursdays. This highly respectable and congenial group of people was organized by a woman named Elizabeth who was president of the historical society until her death in October 2007 and who had a Rialto elementary school named in her honor. The group included two wives of local school board members and a couple of wives of retired business executives. There was also a woman who had retired after many years of teaching high

7

school students, the widow of a man who had taught at a local community college, and a man who once served on the Rialto school board. I never took part in the card games, although I have been very actively involved in the historical society since the late 1980s because of my interest in local history, and I have spent countless hours in the church building.

The group first began their card games in a cozy and secluded room that serves as both den and library in the museum building just north of the church. During a card game, a gray-haired, matronly woman named Betty startled the others when she asked Elizabeth, the president of the historical society, "Do you have ghosts here?" Betty had become convinced the ghost of a girl was in the museum building. The head of the historical society, who spent more time in the building than anyone else, didn't say anything at first, but later remembered that the ashes of a girl named Kristina were kept in the building. Betty, who, along with everyone else present, had never heard about the ashes, immediately concluded that Kristina was the ghost.

Betty never saw Kristina, but said she could hear Kristina's disembodied voice, could strongly feel Kristina's presence, and sensed that Kristina enjoyed playing in a room down the hall from the den which contained late nineteenth and early twentieth century clothes. Betty said Kristina was unhappy much of the time that she was in the church. She also said the ghost was very friendly toward her.

Kristina died at age 11 in 1967 after a long struggle with leukemia. Her family had been members of the church where her ashes are now kept. When the congregation made plans to move to a new church building in the early 1960s, the old church building was going to be auctioned off, which almost certainly would have caused it to be torn down and replaced with a humdrum business building. Kristina's father, a well-known local doctor, bought the church, and donated it to serve as a museum and cultural center. The center was given Kristina's name. Her father, by then retired from his medical practice, lovingly put together a display of her possessions, including artwork, dolls, books, girl scout uniform, schoolwork, etc., in the basement of the church. Her ashes were in a container, disguised as a large book, which was placed with her possessions. The display cabinet is just to the west of the church basement room where the group played their card games. This room is in turn next to a kitchen used to prepare food for various museum events. The base of the stairway that leads up to the main part of the church is next to the display cabinet. .

When I first heard that Betty had told the card players that a ghost was in the building, I didn't take it seriously. I hadn't known about the girl's ashes, even though I was closely associated with the building as the historical society's historian. I figured that any connection between these ashes and the reported ghost had to be due to an overactive imagination. Discovering a ghost by "sensing" or "feeling" its presence seemed even less convincing than clearly seeing one. Obviously, a room could give someone a bad feeling because they felt claustrophobic in it or found its musty odors distasteful. Such a feeling could be blamed on a ghost if one were a believer. Still, the presence of the ashes and the display cabinet of Kristina's possessions made the situation interesting.

Betty considered herself to have psychic abilities and claimed to have had a considerable number of encounters with ghosts during her life, including the spirits of some of her own deceased relatives. She had never mentioned this to the other members of the card-playing group because she didn't want them to suspect she might suffer from delusions. She told me that she had also sensed the presence of other ghosts in the church in addition to Kristina's. She said that one day, when she went to the kitchen in the church's basement to get some food, she was terrified when she sensed the ghost of a woman in her 50s or 60s. The ghost seemed to want her to help Kristina. Betty said, "Get away from me! I don't want anything to do with you!" This response apparently angered Kristina's ghost. Betty said Kristina's ghost seemed friendly to her until she rebuffed the ghost of the woman. Afterward, whenever she encountered Kristina, the girl's ghost would be angry and pouting.

Betty claimed to have discovered a third ghost in the pantry just to the south of the kitchen. She felt this ghost was a woman, but not the same ghost she met in the kitchen. When Betty went into the pantry she became extremely agitated. She felt that something terrible had once happened in the pantry to the person whose ghost lurked there and that the ghost was suffering terribly. She thought the person possibly was murdered in the pantry, although I could find no information that anyone was ever murdered in the church. Betty went into the pantry and announced out loud that she would pray for her. After she had prayed for the ghost, she found she could go into the pantry without experiencing such painful feelings.

Betty claimed that at one point when she arrived to play cards in the basement of the church the room was full of spirits having a party or a meeting. When the other card players started arriving, the ghosts all vanished. She also showed me a large stain on a map that was hanging on a wall in the church basement. It vaguely resembled someone's profile, and Betty thought it might have been made by Kristina or another ghost to send some sort of message.

I did not take these reports of ghosts seriously. After all, the world is full of people who claim supernatural powers, some of whom even make their living from their claim. But my interest increased after additional incidents involving a woman named Denise Werner who joined the group as a regular some months after the card games in the church first started. Denise is a 5'5" slender, pixie-like brunette with gray-green eyes who is younger than most of the other card players. She had not heard any of the stories about ghosts when she joined the card-playing group. To the astonishment of all but Betty, she said, "You are going to think I am crazy, but there are ghosts here!" Denise had concluded that the ghost of a sad little girl was present in the building. Furthermore, she announced that there was a ghost in the pantry and said that she had such a bad feeling when she entered it that she dreaded doing so. She also had a terrible feeling in a storeroom that was near the kitchen, although she wasn't sure if there was actually a ghost in that room. She claimed that she could feel the emotions of the ghosts, but not see them or hear their voices. Betty, in contrast, did not have a bad feeling in the storeroom. There were now two people in the group who were sure that the building was haunted. Was this a scheme to unnerve the other card players? I was interested enough to check into the matter and could find no evidence of collusion.

Denise told me that her three daughters and her mother, grandmother, and great-grandmother all have shown psychic abilities. These ancestors were Cherokee Indians whose powers were greatly respected by other members of the tribe. As I became better acquainted with her she told me that her sensitivity to ghosts often gave her a feeling of terror, and she expressed a wish that she could lose these abilities. Denise said she had her powers to sense spirits since early childhood.

Denise generally didn't tell many people about her ability to sense ghosts. She certainly is no maladjusted mental case, however. She impressed me as a capable person who is respected in the community. She has worked as a volunteer in many community service organizations, often serving as president or secretary. She was a housewife until her children had grown and then she worked for a private investigator, mostly looking into insurance fraud. Her otherworldly powers served her well in making hunches that usually turned out to be uncannily accurate. She is a devout Catholic and does not feel that her mystical abilities are in opposition to her faith. She is used to walking into old buildings and finding ghosts there. Denise loves to travel with her husband and daughters, has been to every continent except the South Pole, and frequently has had hair-raising encounters with ghosts during her visits to historic buildings in other countries.

Although Denise and Betty felt uneasy at times during the card games because of the ghosts they sensed (none of the other card players sensed anything), they enjoyed the games and conversations so much they continued to show up on most Thursdays. During these games Denise felt that Kristina's ghost would sometimes stand by the cabinet containing her possessions and ashes and gaze at her. She found this so unsettling that she would try, at times, to escape Kristina's stare by moving her chair to a location which was not easily seen from the display case. There is a wooden door which separates the card room from the display case and which is usually kept open during the card games. Denise would ask many times for this door to be closed to block her feeling of Kristina's gaze, but she would continue to feel Kristina's presence even with the door closed.

11

In July 1995, a couple of years after Denise first joined the group, they were playing cards on a day when Betty was not able to join them. To the utter amazement of the others, Denise kept going over to the display case and saying, "Go away! Leave me alone! I can't help you!" She told the others that the ghost wanted help. Although it was a very hot summer day, Denise was covered with goose bumps and was shivering. Rex, the only man who played cards with the ladies, told me, "Denise just went crazy. She couldn't possibly have been acting." Denise had always been very composed and self-controlled during card games, and never carried on in such a way before.

A number of days later the other card players were even more amazed when a local newspaper carried an obituary listing the death of Kristina's brother. I later learned that he had taken his own life five days after Denise's outburst. He was born 11 years before Kristina, and lived about 600 miles away from Rialto in Northern California. I knew him when we were both in high school in Rialto and he was one of the most popular kids on campus, generally at the center of the laughing and joking that was going on. At the time of his death he had a wonderful wife, great kids, a successful career as a commercial artist, and a home in the sublime California redwood country. The people I know who were his close friends during his school days were all mystified that he had ended his own life, although I learned that he had a history of depression. His father said he had suffered terrible stress while fighting in Vietnam and had never recovered mentally from those horrors. Denise was particularly shaken by the news of the death of Kristina's brother. She felt that Kristina wanted help during that card game in July, but she had not been able to determine exactly what kind. Now she couldn't help but conclude that Kristina sensed her brother's approaching suicide, and wanted someone to help prevent it.

After hearing about these incidents from several people who were at that July card game (people that I know to be very reliable witnesses), I began for the first time to become seriously interested in the ghost stories. From that time forward, every time a ghostly incident occurred I immediately interviewed everyone involved and took extremely detailed notes.

I later asked Denise what it felt like to sense Kristina's frantic desire for help. She said that when she picks up the emotions of ghosts it feels like they are her own emotions, but she knows they are coming from some other source when there is no reason for her to suddenly be experiencing these emotions. I also asked her what it felt like when she first had sensed Kristina's presence in the church, and she said it was like when you are in a very dark room and you just know that there is somebody else in that room.

On the Thursday one week after Denise's outbursts, the group met at the old church for their next game of cards. During the game Denise announced that Kristina was still upset, but not frantic for help as she was on the previous Thursday. The card games then went on in a routine fashion for the next eight months until another extraordinary incident happened in March 1996. Denise was playing cards and feeling relaxed and happy on that Thursday until Kristina's dad, the retired doctor, came into the building to clean and rearrange Kristina's display case. Denise didn't know him. He had been reasonably well known in town when he was a practicing physician, but by the time she moved to Rialto he had already retired. He closed the wooden door between the display case and the card players and worked for a couple of hours, first picking up the container holding Kristina's ashes to clean its outside. Denise began to lose control again. She was shivering with goose bumps although it was a warm day heated up by the Santa Ana winds. She said she felt sick and might have to go home. She was also crying quietly at times. The doctor was not aware of Denise's reactions.

A half-hour after he left, Denise felt fine again. It was not until after he was gone that someone told Denise he was Kristina's father. The card players were struck by the fact that during the many occasions when Denise played cards in the church she had lost control of herself only twice. The first time happened just before the death of Kristina's brother, and the second occasion came when Kristina's dad arrived to work on her display case. If these were genuine accounts of Kristina's ghost, her appearance in broad daylight went against the old saying that when a rooster crows at daybreak all the ghosts must return to the underworld where they spend the daylight hours. It would

13

become clear to me during future years of ghost watching that there was as much ghostly activity in the daytime hours as at night.

I was tempted to discuss these incidents with Kristina's father, but I did not. There was nothing to gain, since if he did not believe the stories he would think that the museum was catering to a group of nut cases, and if he did believe them he might become very upset. One does not like to upset those who donate buildings to museums.

3   Ghostly Encounters: One Benign and One Terrifying

In January 1997, Elizabeth, the president of the historical society, Jean, the secretary, and I were working on some historical information in the den of the museum building to the north of the old church. Elizabeth was a perfect image of neatness and cleanliness, from her intensely white curls to her impeccably selected clothing and she was the most prolific and effective volunteer in the city's history, working for an enormous variety of civic organizations. She was naturally inclined to reject any suggestion of ghosts since she was very close to someone with Alzheimer's Disease who hallucinated about spirits coming out of walls. She and her sister asked each other, "Which one of us will be the first to see ghosts coming out of walls?" In her job as president, Elizabeth also feared that talk of ghosts in the church could scare off weddings and other fund-raising activities.

Jean Randall, then the secretary of the historical society and now the president, is a lanky, hyper energetic, stylishly attractive, woman who is very "hip" for her age. She is a retired third-grade teacher who has a delightfully biting wit. Like Elizabeth, she is a most credible person.   Jean tells some interesting ghost stories about members of her family, and although she says that she is not sure if they are all true or not, she is convinced that at least one of them is. When her husband was terminally ill with lung cancer in Rialto, their daughter, Karen, a teacher who lives in Oregon, would pray for him each evening. Karen noticed the sound of an owl as she prayed, and told a fellow teacher about this. The other teacher told her there is a Native American legend that when someone dies an owl comes to take the soul away.

When the end was nearing for her father, Karen came to Rialto. The first evening of her visit, she went out onto the patio of her parents' house and was astounded to hear an owl. She told her mother, who said they had not heard an owl for many years. Karen then told Jean about the owl she had heard in Oregon while praying for her father and the Indian legend that an owl comes to take a dying person's soul away. Each evening that she was there Karen and Jean would sit on the patio and listen to the sounds of the owl. Karen's father died on Mother's Day, and she and Jean were wondering if they would hear the owl that evening. They did not. Because of this experience Jean was more inclined to accept the idea that ghosts could be in the church than Elizabeth was.

While Elizabeth, Jean, and I were working in the den, I heard a soft female voice speaking for a few seconds out in the hallway. This seemed odd since the place was locked and no one else was there. I could not make out the words. I said to Elizabeth, "Who is that?" She replied, "So you heard it too. I heard it earlier." I went out into the hallway and there was no one there. I looked around the rest of the building, and except for the three of us it was empty of people. I would have thought it was just a product of my imagination if Elizabeth had not heard it too. Strangely, Jean didn't hear this very audible voice. Later, when a real-life spirit investigator came to our museum, he said it was common that one or more people in a group might experience a manifestation, but others might not because of differences in ability to sense such things. Could this be the explanation, or did Jean just not hear the voice?

We were working in a location where the voice could not have come from outside the building. It was speaking in normal tones, and when one is working in the den it is only possible to hear voices from outside the building if they are yelling. I even conducted an experiment by talking quite loudly but not yelling outside the building. Nobody in the den could hear me. Could the sound of the voice have resulted from a prank, such as someone leaving a tape player or other electronic sound-making device triggered to play for a few seconds in the building while we were working in the den? Since this was a spur-of-the-moment meeting nobody other than the three of us even knew we were going to meet, and I am certain that neither Elizabeth nor Jean, who never play a practical joke on anyone, would ever do such a thing.

When I first heard the voice I thought someone could have entered the locked building. It simply did not occur to me that Elizabeth and I might have heard a ghost. Only after searching everywhere without finding anyone did I recall Betty's claims of hearing Kristina's disembodied voice. This gave me an eerie "do you

16

suppose?"feeling, but I still felt there must be some other explanation for the origin of the voice.

In April 1997 I came across another ghost story having to do with the museum. An ex- Rialto policeman who is now a private investigator came to see Elizabeth at the historical society to get some information. As they were talking he suddenly asked her, "Do you know you may have a ghost in your building?" He told her a story about a terrifying encounter he had when he and his partner answered a burglar alarm at the old church and saw the apparition of a female in the basement of the church. Since I heard this story from Elizabeth rather than from the ex-policeman, I had no chance to ask him any questions. I thought, as did Elizabeth, that if they saw such an apparition it must have been the ghost of Kristina. The policeman had asked Elizabeth never to reveal his name or the name of his partner, since policemen are not supposed to see ghosts while investigating possible burglaries. We continued to assume the policeman saw Kristina until I finally had a chance to interview the man about the incident on December 5, 1997. I will refer to him as Ned, although that is not his real name.

Ned answered the burglar alarm with his partner during the graveyard shift, sometime between 11 PM and 4 AM. They walked around the outside of the church and saw that no windows had been smashed in and then went inside and found that nobody was in the main part of the church. They then went down the stairway to the basement shining their flashlights. There was a small ceiling light on in the basement and they saw that nobody was there. When they turned to start back up the stairs they saw an apparition standing at the base of the stairway. At the instant they saw her, Ned said the room instantly became as cold as a freezer. He said the woman was about 35 to 40 years old and he was certain that she was wearing a turn-of-the century Victorian mourning dress.

He described her as wearing a black veil, which barely reached below her eyes. It hung down on either side of her head and rested on her shoulders like a scarf. The dress was black and had a high waist. The sleeves reached to about two inches above where the hand joined the wrist and the ends of the sleeves were covered with white brocaded material. There was also a little white at the top of the dress where the collar gathered.

The dress went straight down to about eighteen inches above the floor. The woman had no feet. She was floating above the floor, although the image was steady and was not bouncing about. Initially she was looking down, as though she was staring at their flashlights, but then she looked up and began to stare directly at them. They saw her blink when she first looked up. Ned said he could see "every infinitesimal detail of her." He remembered her eyebrows, and described her features as sharp, straight, and almost chiseled. Her skin had color and was not pasty. Despite all of the details of her image that could be seen, she was transparent and he could see through her. She made no sound.

Ned went on to say that he and his partner were standing about eight feet from her and she just stared at them for about fifteen or twenty seconds. They tried to approach her more closely and she instantly vanished. They didn't see her disappear. She was just gone.

He described the experience as being extremely frightening. They went upstairs where they met Elizabeth, who was called in the middle of the night by the police department to let them in the church. She asked if they had seen anyone in the building, and they said everything was okay, never mentioning the strange sight that they had seen. Later, Ned got a message from his partner to meet him at a nearby cafe. The partner was badly shaken by seeing the ghost, but he let Ned know he was not about to admit seeing it. Ned's partner said, "I don't want to go see Uncle Bob." When the police department was unsure about the mental state of one of their officers, they sent him, or her, to a psychiatrist popularly known as Uncle Bob.

Ned thought this event took place about 1989 or 1990, but his description of the large amounts of supplies being stored in the basement made Elizabeth think it must have been in 1986. This was the year she became president of the Rialto Historical Society, and began to work to get the stored materials out of the church basement. This would have been a couple of years before Kristina's ashes were moved to the church from a mausoleum in nearby San Bernardino.

Despite the fact that the incident happened so many years before Ned told me about it, he seemed to have amazingly detailed recall of it. He said he was sure he could recognize the face of the ghost if he ever saw a photograph of her. Her image must have been permanently burned into his memory. He said he had been in combat and you would not think he would be scared of a ghost, but the apparition caused him such terrible fear that he said he experienced a feeling of terror just while telling me about it. He said he never wanted to go into the old church at night again.

Almost 5 years later, in August 2002, I was to meet another policeman who had a very similar experience to Ned's. By then I had taken Elizabeth's place as the sucker who was called to go to the church when the alarm sounded in the middle of the night. I told the man who called me that I would go to the church, meet the Rialto Police there, and see if anyone had broken in. I arrived before the police, and walked around the buildings. I saw no evidence of a break in, and then I went into the church and museum buildings to see if everything was okay. I found both alarms were set when I entered. I reset them when I left and locked both buildings.

When I walked to the front of the church, I saw two policemen. I told them that everything seemed to be all right. The biggest of the two policemen said, "We won't have to go into the church, unless you ask us to have a look around." I was surprised to see how scared he seemed about the idea of going into the church. I was sure there was no need to go into the church, but for some reason I said, "Let's go inside and have a look."

When we entered the church from the sidewalk off Second Street, the big policeman said, nervously, "This is the way we came in before." I wondered what he was talking about. As we entered the large basement room, he said, "I don't want you to think I am crazy, but when I came with another policeman to investigate a burglar alarm years ago we saw a figure here."

I was very interested now, asking, "What did the figure look like and where did you see it?" He said it was a woman wearing an old dress that "looked like it came from the time of the Civil War." He said the dress was white and looked torn, or else it may have been covered with lace. He said she had white or gray hair, and looked like a hologram. The other policeman said, "You mean she looked like something from the Haunted House at Disneyland?" The policeman who had seen the ghost said yes. He said she was transparent, had no feet, and floated up the stairs, but they heard her footsteps. He said the image of her was very white.

I asked when this had happened, and he said that he thought it must have been around 1992. He told me that the policeman with him at the time had said, "Did you see what I saw?" The other policeman later said, "I'm not going to tell anyone about this. I don't want people to think I am crazy."

The policeman who had seen the ghost years before was clearly scared. He said he didn't think he had been that scared when he actually saw the ghost, but coming back to the site had given him very bad feelings. I told them that the building was haunted for sure, and mentioned that I had notebooks full of ghost stories. The policeman who had told the story about the ghost looked startled, and told his companion, "See, I told you." They both looked surprised when I told them how delighted I was that the burglar alarm had gone off so I could hear this story.

I asked the policeman who had told the ghost story if he would give me his name, promising not to reveal it. I told him how another policeman had told me years before of a similar encounter with a ghost that he and his partner had experienced at the base of the same stairs. This encounter apparently happened around 1986. I said that I had promised not to reveal the names of those other two policemen, and I never had. The two policemen who came on August 10, 2002 were startled to hear about the earlier encounter the ghost had with two other members of the police force. The nervous policeman hesitated for a long time before he told me his name. He and his partner went no farther than the basement room, and soon were on their way out of the building.

Years before when the other policeman told me about the ghost he and his partner encountered at the base of the stairs late at night, he said the ghost had been dressed in black with white trim. This was in contrast to the woman in the white dress the second pair of policemen had seen. The woman the first pair saw instantly disappeared as they looked at her, rather than going up the stairs. Even though the color of the dress varied in the two stories, it sounded a lot like the same ghost. Now that I had heard that four Rialto Policemen had seen her, I wondered how many others had too. Elizabeth, the late president of our historical society, thought this might have been the reason that the police were so hesitant to search through the building when the alarm goes off.

Returning once again to 1997, five years before I was to hear the second policeman's ghost story, neither Denise nor Betty had ever sensed the presence of the Victorian lady, even though they noticed other ghosts than Kristina. With the addition of ex-policeman Ned's tale of encountering the lady ghost in the black dress at the base of the stairs, I began to wonder whether there might be people who could help us with this mystery. We were clearly in over our heads. Were there perhaps real-life ghost investigators who could be invited in to help us? I asked Elizabeth and Jean what they would think about getting such a person to come to the church. They both said it sounded like fun. At this point we still didn't really believe in ghosts, but thought we could maybe get to the bottom of these incidents.

I arranged for a ghost investigator who has an office in a nearby city to come to our museum to see what he would conclude. I got his name from a ninety-year-old woman who had been a ghost investigator for many decades and who has written a book about ghosts. She seemed to find the subject of ghosts very boring. When I asked if she would like to hear the details of the ghostly activities in our church, she said, "No, I know so many stories about ghosts you couldn't tell me anything I haven't heard before." She told me to call a man named Tom Hagman who she said was very psychic. When I called him and told him that we might have a haunted building on our hands he agreed to come take a look. He asked me not to tell him any details about the haunting because that might prejudice his investigation. None of us expected to hear anything that made a lot of sense to us when he came. But we were excited about the prospect of his visit anyway. None of us had ever met a real ghost buster.

At the time Tom Hagman had a very successful vocational rehabilitation business. However, his avocation and true love has long been research in parapsychology. He has spent over 30 years investigating everything from reported hauntings to extra sensory perception. He has done a great deal of lecturing and teaching in parapsychology. Sometimes he is paid and sometimes not for his investigations, but he generously donated his time to do this study for us. He describes himself as a mystic.

4   Tom Hagman

On a balmy spring evening in May 1997, I was standing in the

parking lot of the old church, eagerly waiting for the arrival of the spirit investigator. Soon, I saw a big, new, shiny, opalescent, Lincoln Town car turn off the nearby main street of town and pull into the parking lot. Tom Hagman stepped out of the car and introduced himself, and, for some reason, I immediately had the impression of a minister. About six feet tall and stocky, bespectacled, in his early 50s, and impeccably neat, he spoke with a very gentle and soothing voice. He was accompanied by an efficient assistant named Judi Kuykendall. Tom introduced himself by immediately saying that he had seen a little girl looking down at him from the upper windows of the church, which was then still locked with the burglar alarm set. Later, he was to say she was smiling and she looked as if she was expecting him. He announced that she was wearing a dress with a round collar, and when I asked him how old she was, he said eleven or twelve (Kristina died at the age of eleven). My first impression of him was astonishment, because true to his wishes, I had not told him that a little girl was suspected of haunting the church.

He demonstrated his desire to get down to business by requesting immediate entrance to the church before the little ghost could hide. While we were unlocking the door and disarming the burglar alarm, he removed some boxes from his car and brought them inside. Among other items, the boxes contained an instrument to measure temperature (he said spirits are associated with a cold spot), a small hand-held pendulum that he said could show the presence of a ghost because the energy associated with the spirit could cause the pendulum to move, a Polaroid camera, a thirty-five mm camera, a tape recorder, and a slate board and chalk in case a spirit wanted to write something. He did admit that only once had a spirit wanted to write something on the slate board.

He started looking around the church, and soon summoned us to come up from the basement to the pews in the main part of the church. He said the ghost was at the piano on the stage in front of the pews, and he could "psychically" hear piano music (Kristina had taken piano lessons). We heard nothing. He said his temperature sensor measured a cold spot, and his pendulum started moving, both showing she was there. He had his assistant take photographs of both the stage and piano.

Tom then hurried around the hallways at the back of the church, saying the spirit was running around this area playing and laughing. This amazed Elizabeth, the president of the historical society, because she recalled that Betty (the first of the card players to have sensed that a ghost was present) said the little girl's spirit spent her time running around and playing. After spending some time in the church, Tom said he heard the little ghost say, "It was an accident." One of the people present while Tom was investigating speculated that Kristina might have been referring to her brother's death.

He then went back downstairs to the church basement, where he claimed to have "psychically" seen a small rocking chair in the basement start to rock. He told me I probably wouldn't be able to see the motion (I didn't) but that Kristina likes to sit on this chair. After spending some time in this area he said the ghost loved her grandmother, who is also deceased, very much, and looked for her grandma in the church at times. Elizabeth, who remembers both

Kristina and Kristina's grandmother, remarked that Kristina was crazy about her grandmother. He also said that he had heard the ghost sob at times when she was lonely.

Tom then went over to a room just to the south of the display case where Kristina's ashes and possessions are kept. This room contains a number of toys, and Tom claimed that it has especially strong energy, showing it is a favorite place for Kristina to go. The base of the stairway is just to the north of the display case and Tom said he heard the ghost's voice there when he first started up the stairway, although he could not make out the words. He also said he saw Kristina go through the wall by her display case out of the corner of his eye. He said she frequently went through the wall there. When Tom made the statement about Kristina passing through the wall by her display case he had not been told that the objects in the glass case were her personal possessions or that her ashes were in the case. He didn't even learn until the end of his first visit to the church that the building was named after Kristina. He had only been told that the church and museum were the Rialto Historical Society.

Our ghost expert certainly was not wasting any time. I happily followed him as he walked around the remainder of the church basement, particularly watching as he approached the pantry to see if he would sense anything there. Betty thought that the ghost of a woman was in this room, and Denise sensed the presence of a ghost there too.

Tom's eyes widened as he stepped into the pantry. He said, "I have a feeling like electricity going through my body when I am near a spirit, and there is one moving around in here." I asked him if it was Kristina and he said, "No, it is another spirit that is disgruntled. It would like you people to get out of here. But you shouldn't worry about it because it does not have enough power to do any harm to you." He left his tape recorder running in the pantry and closed the door. Tom had heard nothing about the claims that the pantry was haunted by a different ghost than Kristina (I had thought that this conclusion sounded totally ridiculous), and I was dumbfounded to hear him come to the same conclusion. Or had Tom, and Betty and Denise at earlier times, experienced an uncomfortable feeling due to something about the nature of the pantry---a claustrophobic feeling or an unpleasant reaction to a subtle odor of the room, for example--- which they mistakenly attributed to a ghost in the room? The pantry is a very neat, clean, and pleasant little room that doesn't give me any bad feelings, and I don't see how the room could cause anyone to feel uncomfortable.

After Tom came out of the pantry, he walked around the adjacent kitchen, and remarked that he also had an uncomfortable feeling when he was standing in front of the stove. Tom then walked to the storage room that is a short distance northwest of the kitchen (this area was formerly the boiler room), and said this room also gave him very bad feelings. This storage area also gives Denise a terrible feeling of dread, although Betty did not have any bad feelings in it. Tom, like Denise, was not sure his feelings were due to a ghost in the storeroom. But if not a ghost what? The storeroom seems completely innocuous to me. I certainly do not remember having any negative feelings when in it. Our mini-procession then walked around through the newer building to the north of the old church that serves as the main body of our museum, and Tom said he could sense nothing in there. He concluded that Kristina confines her activities mostly to the upper and lower portions of the back of the church.

Tom had successfully astounded us by giving us a series of observations that agreed with things we had heard from other witnesses of our reported ghosts, or with things we knew about Kristina. Half a dozen of us connected with the museum were there to watch him (neither Betty nor Denise were present), and all of us were open-mouthed with trembling with disbelief and excitement. We took turns laughing at the expressions on each other's faces. I do not ever remember feeling as astonished, and my non-believing museum colleagues were obviously feeling similar emotions.

Tom did no probing of our knowledge, either overtly or surreptitiously, as he was carrying out his investigation and stating his observations. As he requested, we did not give him our accounts of the ghostly happenings until after he finished making his own investigation and told us his conclusions. He asked no questions to elicit information from us before stating his conclusions, and his conclusions were direct statements and not hedged in the form of questions. Neither was it a matter of him making both right and wrong statements, and having us remember the hits and forget the misses. I listened very carefully and took very detailed notes, and he simply did not make any statements that were in conflict with what Denise and Betty had told us or with other information that we had.

He told us that he was sure he could communicate with Kristina, but, since a wedding rehearsal was just starting upstairs, it would not be a good time, because he was sensitive to the reactions of people seeing him apparently talking to nobody. His impression was that Kristina did not want to leave, so we had plenty of time for our investigation. He was more than willing to return whenever we wanted him to talk with Kristina and find out more. He gave us a hint of what we might expect by telling us some of the remarkable things that happened when he holds what he called a "spirit communication." Completely unexpected spirits often related to the people at the session frequently turn up. This seemed like something we should not miss, and we invited him to do a spirit communication in the church.

A few days later, Tom told me over the phone that when the thirty-five mm camera photographs of the stage and piano were developed they showed a strange green mist in the area where he believed the ghost to be. He said that although he has tried many times to photograph a ghost, he has never succeeded, and in fact the purported photographs of ghosts he has seen look like double exposures to him.

Neither did the tape recording in the pantry contain any evidence. I asked Tom if he ever recorded the voice of a ghost, and he told me a story about how he once captured a very startling ghostly voice on tape. A man had called him and claimed to be tormented by spirits. Tom agreed to meet him, and when he did so found that the man was dressed entirely in black, and drove a truck painted inside and out in black. He said he did this to try get rid of evil spirits, because wherever he went, the spirits were there. Tom talked to the man for 20 or 30 minutes in his truck with a tape recorder running. Tom said, "If you want them to go, go to a Catholic Church, call on a higher power, and tell them to leave." The man agreed to do so.

When Tom played the tape back and reached the point where he was telling the man to go to a Catholic Church, he heard a hissing voice on the tape say, "You son of a bitch!" Tom said this menacing voice, which he didn't hear during the original conversation, turned his blood to water. The bedeviled man, who was listening to the tape with Tom, said, "See!" After the man left, Tom never saw him again. Tom put the tape in his car, and it disappeared forever when his car was stolen a few days later. I loved the story, but I was not convinced by it. I was still looking for hard evidence.

We arranged with Tom to hold a spirit communication on Tuesday, June 17, 1997 at 6 PM. There was an open house, luncheon, and fashion show of the old clothes in our museum on the Saturday before the spirit communication. The fashion show models had a rehearsal a day or two before the show and Denise was one of the models. The fashion show was to be upstairs in the main part of the old church, a place where Denise had never been before, since she had only been present at the card games in the downstairs church basement room. When she came upstairs, Elizabeth decided to run a little experiment of her own

She began to steer Denise to places in the church Tom had seen, heard, or otherwise sensed the ghost. Neither Elizabeth nor anyone else told Denise the details of Tom's earlier investigation of the historical society buildings. Her experiment yielded instant results. When she walked Denise to the room where Tom first saw Kristina looking out the upstairs window, Denise reacted with horror and refused to go in. Out of the several rooms behind the altar, this one seemed particularly abhorrent to her. Elizabeth continued to take Denise around the main part of the church and finally brought her to the piano where Tom said a cold spot showed that Kristina had been seated at the piano and playing it. The instant Denise reached the piano Denise began to shiver and said, "I feel so cold here!" Elizabeth and the other members of the group saw her begin to shiver and noticed goose bumps break out on her arms. The location did not feel at all cold to the other people in the party. After Denise's experiences in going around the church, Elizabeth told her about Tom's observations.

It took a lot of talking to convince Denise to come to the spirit communication. Elizabeth kept trying to talk her into coming, and Denise would say it sounded very interesting, but she had great anxieties about being there. Denise talked to Betty about the spirit communication (Betty and her husband moved to Irvine, California some time before I first contacted Tom), and Betty advised her not to go. Betty said she would be terrified of attending a spirit communication herself. Finally, Rex Wiltse, a former Rialto school board member and the only man who played cards with the ladies on Thursdays, asked Denise to come and she agreed to be there. Denise said if the spirit communication bothered her too much, she would leave. Even though Betty would not be attending, we would have at least one of the original ghost discoverers at our meeting.

I was very curious to know more about Tom, and wondered if he had some sort of training in parapsychology. I learned that he has a bachelor's degree in sociology from California State University at San Bernardino, and he has gathered most of his knowledge about psychic matters from his own experiences. I found out that he is a very avid collector, and loves to dabble in antiques. He has a collection of over 200 Santa Claus figures, some of which even play music and dance. He gives interesting lectures about the history and evolution of Santa Claus when invited to speak to groups. Tom looks like a younger Santa Claus although he lacks a beard.

Tom is also the President of the Parapsychology Association of Riverside (PAR), and has held that position for 18 years of the association's existence. PAR is a non-profit educational and research organization in the field of paranormal research. Tom spends most of his free time driving from city to city and helping people with an incredible variety of problems. These can range from removal of ghosts from their houses to counseling them about personal problems, such as inconsolable grieving over the loss of a loved one or dealing with severe marital problems. He also meets with many people just to assist them in exploring widely varied aspects of the paranormal. These gifts of help and/or psychic exploration that he travels around bestowing, most often for free, make him seem like a sort of Santa Claus to a multitude of people who have received them. Tom became a minister so that he could legally perform counseling, and he conducted church services for a number of years, stopped for a period of time, and then has begun conducting them again in recent years. Currently he is the Spiritual Leader for the Unity Church of the Crossroads in Riverside, California. Over a long period of time, he has accumulated an enormous number of extremely devoted friends, who are all impressed by his genuine sincerity, and most are amazed by his abilities. He always seems to be very mellow, and people find him very pleasant as well as interesting to be around. Surprisingly, he told me that his best friend is a total skeptic, who is convinced that there is no existence beyond the material world.

Tom is very happily married to a beautiful, young, dark-haired, dark-eyed, very feminine woman named Jan. He claims that she is very psychic. They are always collaborating on projects that fascinate them both. Jan is an optometrist, with a degree from the Southern California College of Optometry. She has a bachelor's degree in the biological sciences from the University of California at Irvine, where she had a 3.7 grade point average in her core courses (I am including these mentions of university backgrounds to counter the idea that believers in ghosts are uneducated, ignorant people). Jan is also an enthusiastic collector. She is fascinated by the British Royalty, and has a very large collection of Royal memorabilia, including many items from coronations. Jan also has a collection of 75 angels. She loves to give authentic old-fashioned tea parties, with all the proper china, scones, food, etc. She charges money to attend the tea parties, and then donates it to charitable causes. Tom said that Jan would come to our next ghost investigation session.

5   The Spirit Communication

When Denise arrived for the spirit communication, she had painted a streak of white on one of her cheeks, and wore a Cherokee Indian jacket and Cherokee jewelry, undoubtedly to connect with her psychic Cherokee forebears. Tom came with his assistant, Judi, and with his wife, Jan.

Initially, Tom was concerned by the number of people who showed up for the spirit communication, as he thought it might be too large a group to get good results. There were eight people at his first investigation of the old church, and seven of those eight came for the spirit communication along with six people who weren't there on the previous occasion. But, both Denise and Tom said they liked the number thirteen---the number of people who showed up.

We were all very intrigued by the idea of a spirit communication but somewhat skeptical.   It was a new experience for all of us, so Tom began by telling us how it would be conducted. Everyone would sit in an oval pattern and hold hands to form an "energy ring." During the spirit communication everyone was supposed to keep their eyes closed at all times and not to tell about their own experiences until it was over. Tom said if we didn't close our eyes, we would be distracted by our surroundings, and less able to have the other-dimensional communication we were seeking.   He would do most of the talking and convey messages from Kristina. Other people at the spirit communication could occasionally ask questions or make remarks. Everyone was supposed to imagine a great column of brilliant white light rotating in a counterclockwise direction, with the energy rotating right through our bodies. This was said to be for our own protection. During all the time we were holding hands in a ring, Tom's assistant, Judi, was sitting at a separate table writing down everything that was said. Tom was later to tell me our spirit communication was not a seance, because a true seance would have the medium in a trance, and the medium in a true seance would try to conjure up an apparition.

Doesn't this sound like a lot of pseudoscientific nonsense that should totally discredit Tom's investigation?   Holding hands in an "energy ring"? Keeping our eyes closed? Tom alone conveying messages from Kristina? An assistant free to aid Tom's "magic"? Pseudoscientific nonsense or not, we were about to have some very strange experiences. Even I was to have my skepticism rattled.

Shortly before the session was to start, I heard the sound of someone knocking loudly on a door that opens at the base of a short series of steps leading down at the southeast corner of the old church. We had been expecting a woman named Barbara to arrive, and assumed that this was she. A man went to open the door for her and was surprised to find no one was there. He went up to the adjacent parking lot and sidewalk, looked around, and saw no one in any direction. We never were to see Barbara. Later, I learned she had not come because she was "a little bit afraid." Could the knocking at the door have been some kids playing a prank and then running off? When we discussed this later, Tom said he didn't think so. For one thing, we would have expected to hear the muffled sound of the kids' feet running up the stairs as they made their getaway. An even stronger reason that Tom didn't think this was due to pranksters was because some of the people at the spirit communication did not hear the knocking. But I did!

I was amazed to learn the woman sitting next to me did not hear the knocking, since I know she has very good hearing, as does another woman in the group who was also certain she did not hear the knocking sound at the door. She heard someone say, "That must be Barbara," and saw a man go to open the door, but she never heard the knocking. She was waiting for the session to begin and not talking to anyone at the time she saw the others react to the knocking. We took a quick poll and three of the thirteen people present did not hear the knocking sounds. Some people who heard the sounds thought the knocking took place against the door while others had the impression someone was tapping on the window by the door.

A series of additional, very audible or loud, and very different sounds were to follow, each of which were to be heard by some people but not by others. Tom told us that this was evidence of ghostly activity since some people have more psychic ability than others, and will detect a manifestation while others present at the same time will not. Supernatural activity before our session was even to begin?

The next sound I heard occurred a few minutes later. It was a very loud "pop" that came from the north end of the room, the opposite end of the room from the sidewalk and street outside. This was not the normal creaking or cracking sound one hears in an old building or house, but was much louder. The spirit communication session had not started yet, and I heard Tom mention the loud sound to Judi. But, Judi had not heard it. Only Tom, Denise, and I heard the loud noise. The others looked very surprised when they were told about this sound they did not hear. Tom later compared the noise to the sound of a two-by-four breaking. It was extremely loud. I was astounded that none of the other ten people heard this sound. I was further astounded that I was now apparently lumped in with Tom and Denise, and I did not even have a white streak on my cheek!

The next noise occurred after the spirit communication meeting had started, and it was a whooshing noise that oscillated up and down in pitch and went on for a long time. It sounded like it was coming from above our heads. After the session, one woman said it was like the whooshing sound of a rope swinging around in a circular motion overhead. This description matches the sound I heard quite well although the noise was louder than the sound of a twirling rope. Denise and Tom heard this sound too. Denise described it as a wind-like sound. The rope-twirling sound was loud enough that it seemed impossible to me that anyone with anywhere near normal hearing would not have heard it. Why did nine of the thirteen people present not recall hearing it?

The last sound in the series of different sounds I heard was someone sobbing, not loudly but certainly very audibly. After the session was over, and before I had the chance to mention that I heard the sound of crying, a woman said she had heard the sound of someone sobbing. Only three out of the thirteen people present recalled the sobbing. This time, neither Tom nor Denise seemed to hear the sound. Tom did hear something that sounded like birds singing, and said he saw an image of Kristina at the same time. Denise also heard the sounds of birds singing. She thought they sounded like mourning doves. The rest of us did not remember such a sound.

Could this selective recall in such cases as the whooshing, rope-twirling sound and the sobbing sound have happened because we didn't discuss these sounds until the session was over? Had some people forgotten what they heard after going through all of the other experiences of the spirit communication? These sounds occurred at a time when people were attentively listening to see what would happen next, and I know the people who were there well enough to say with certainty that those who heard nothing all have good hearing and good memories. I will never forget these eerie sounds I heard at the spirit communication, and I am sure those who didn't recall hearing them would never have forgotten them either had they indeed heard them.

Tom was later to say he has heard other spirit communications open with strange unworldly noises, although not the same sounds we heard. He said it was like a door opening between the two different worlds to begin communication, and the strange sounds that can be heard by some but not by others immediately grab people's attention, as if to give a message that this is serious stuff. He said this could happen by itself, and Kristina might not have caused it.

Some parapsychology researchers have claimed convincing evidence of what has generally been reported as small but statistically significant amounts of ESP in laboratory settings. This has been disputed by other investigators who have carried out similar experiments and concluded that they saw absolutely no evidence of ESP. Scientists in general are very dubious of the possibility of extrasensory perception. We had just been exposed to a series of sounds, ranging from clearly audible to very loud to those that heard them, which were completely inaudible to a considerable number of people with excellent hearing. This seemed to be an extremely powerful demonstration of ESP. This was incredible---evidence of ghosts and ESP at the same time!

At the beginning of the spirit communication, Tom asked if there was a particular question anyone wanted to ask. Since no one responded, he commented that he felt there was someone present who had a knee problem, and did that person have a question or something to say. Elizabeth said she had a bad knee, and then asked, "Is Kristina happy here?"

An aside is in order here. Obviously the odds were good that someone in the group had a knee problem, so Tom got no high grade for extrasensory ability here. But Elizabeth said after the session that when her bad knee was mentioned she felt something brush lightly against the top of it, like the feeling when one of her cats brushes against her. This caused a feeling that spread clear down to her foot. She was amazed by this sensation. Could someone have reached over and brushed the top of Elizabeth's knee when everyone's eyes were closed? I am certain this did not happen. Everyone seated in the oval pattern, including Tom, was continually holding hands with the person on each side of them, and Judi, who was taking notes rather than holding hands, was at a table at some distance to the north of the group.

The nearest people to Elizabeth were my cousin, Skip Sapp, on her left, and his wife, Anne Sapp, on her right. I am sure that neither of them, both retired teachers of impeccable character and honesty, brushed the top of her knee. Also, I frequently opened my eyes to see that nothing funny was going on (I am, after all, a scientist). I never saw anyone else whose eyes were open except for Judi. I asked Elizabeth if she ever had a similar feeling when she couldn't see anything brushing against the top of her knee, and she said she sometimes felt pain but never any feeling like that without something actually touching her.

In answer to Elizabeth's question, Tom stated that Kristina wanted to leave the church but had resolved that she must stay for her dad's sake. The next question was asked by Connie, a beautiful woman who once had won the title of "Miss Rialto". Her question was "Could she contact her mother?" She was thinking that Kristina's mother, who died a few years before, could come and take Kristina away.

Immediately after she asked this question, Connie said she got zapped. She had trouble describing what she experienced, since she had never felt anything like it before. She described it as a "passing, all-enveloping energy flow through her body from left to right." I was holding her left hand and felt nothing. She said it was very strong, and although she felt it most strongly through her shoulders and upper body, she could feel it all over her body. She said it lasted only for a split second, although time seemed to slow down when it happened. Immediately after this experience, Connie recalled hearing someone (my notes show it was Tom's wife, Jan) quote Kristina as saying, "You are not my mother."

Tom conveyed conversations between Kristina and Denise during the spirit communication, and at one point Tom said Kristina came over to Denise, who was sitting to the right of Connie. It was speculated that the remark, "You are not my mother," was directed by Kristina at Denise, because she may have confused Denise with her mother, or because she resented Denise acting like her mother. At that time, Connie said she thought Kristina passed through her body on her way to Denise and caused the strange feelings.

Elizabeth pointed out that Connie looked much more like Kristina's mother than Denise or anyone else present. Later, when Connie had a chance to consider these things at more length, she remembered Elizabeth's remark, and decided Kristina might have confused her with her mother, especially after Connie said, as though she were speaking of herself in the third person, "Could she contact her mother?" Connie thought Kristina might then have examined her closely, zapping her in the process, and then made the remark that Connie was not her mother. It was a strange incident, since Tom and Jan certainly did not know Kristina's mother resembled Connie, and yet the remark, "You are not my mother," was quoted at a time that made it fit in very logically with Connie's strange experience.

The exchanges between Kristina and Denise began with Denise saying she thought Kristina was irritated with her, because Kristina believed Denise was capable of communicating with her but refused. She explained that before a recent heart operation she had not felt well, was easily irritated by any little disturbance, and had shut out Kristina's attempts to communicate with her. She promised not to do this in the future. Tom said Kristina was apologizing to Denise for affecting Denise's breathing. Denise said Kristina caused her to breath very rapidly (none of us had heard this before), and she would stop doing it in the future.

As to Kristina not leaving the church, Tom said that one of her reasons was that her dad had been very domineering with her, and she believed she would be breaking his rules if she left to go on. She said she wanted to communicate with Denise because she felt that she would understand her situation since Denise had a similar childhood. Denise acknowledged to us that she had a very strict upbringing. I had never heard this about Denise, and I am sure that Tom didn't know the details of Denise's childhood. Tom quoted Kristina as saying another reason she couldn't leave now was because she feared it would cause problems with her dad's health, because he might be developing heart problems. Kristina's dad had previously told us that his father and brother died of a rare form of heart disease and he thought he was developing it too. Tom could not have known this. Tom said Kristina also concluded she couldn't leave until her dad knew "it's not his fault."

Kristina apparently said that she was unable to reach her mother while she was in the church. It was something she wanted to do, but she just couldn't do it. Kristina said her grandmother was someone who could influence her father, but when Jan asked if her grandmother could intervene, Tom gave Kristina's answer as NO!

Tom said there was something Kristina wanted to write to her dad in color with crayons or colored pencils. She liked color, as could be seen from the display case, which contains many of her colored drawings. Whenever paper and pencils were used in the church basement, she had a great urge to write. She became very active at those times. Tom said she said, "John," (apparently referring to me because she knew I write) and told me that she wanted to write. She apparently then repeated "John, John," and said the one thing her father would accept was writing. Tom asked if I ever experienced her writing through me. I told him I had never written anything I did not intend to write, except for typos. He said, "Maybe she will work her problems out through you.

Other very strange things happened when the spirit communication was underway. One woman would wait four months before telling that she had sensed the silhouette of a person in front of brilliant white light as she sat with her eyes closed. She couldn't see enough detail to distinguish any identifying features, and she felt that this experience seemed so contrived she didn't even tell us about it at the time. But finally Tom said, "I can't do anymore. We may need more than one session." The spirit communication was over. Tom looked quite drained for a few minutes after the session, but then recovered his normal appearance. Denise was sweating profusely and had to leave the room for a while to seek a cooler area. She said that normally she feels chills when she interacts with Kristina, and this was the first time she experienced such a feeling of intense overheating. She also said she thought she would not experience a feeling of dread when she was around Kristina in the future. Tom said Denise might be a natural medium and that such people experience intense feelings of heat when they work with spirits. Finally he apologized for not finding a way to send Kristina on her way out of the church.

Later, I asked Jan Hagman if she was able to see Kristina, and Jan told me she could see Kristina's hair, the shape of her face, the shape and size of her body, and her clothes, but she couldn't see the features of her face. Jan said this is typically the way ghosts appear to her, although she can sometimes clearly see their faces. Jan added that she can sense the emotions of ghosts, and often hear them.

Tom told us that he was sure the disgruntled spirit in the pantry was a man who had no relationship to Kristina. Jan reported hearing the word "caretaker" when the spirit in the pantry was discussed. Elizabeth recalled that between the time that the church was no longer in use and the time it was converted to a museum, a couple were hired as caretakers, and they stole all sorts of valuable fixtures and other things. It was speculated that if this man had died his spirit might now be in the pantry.

Obviously if an attempt was made to send this second spirit on its way, it would have to be done another time. Tom reported that Kristina was scared of the spirit in the pantry and avoided that location. Both Tom and Denise speculated that whoever was in the pantry might have played a role in blocking Kristina from leaving. Tom also said it was hard on him to act as a channel, and he rarely did it. He said he was willing to make this effort for Kristina.

After the spirit communication, Tom asked if his wife, Jan, could have a tour of the old church. Elizabeth took Jan, Tom, and Judi up into the main part of the church. Judi said that when they were there, she felt impelled, for some reason, to leave the group and walk down the center aisle of the church toward the piano on the stage in front of the pews. When she was part way down the aisle, she stopped, and suddenly felt a chill feeling. She then felt something like a current move through her body, though, she said, not as unpleasant and frightening as a current of electricity. The current gave her a breathless feeling. Tom came along just then, and said, "There is something here!" Tom said this before Judi had a chance to tell him what she experienced. Judi thought Kristina had passed through her body.

At this point, we were all willing and eager to have Tom come back in the future to make another effort to free Kristina and find out more about the spirit in the pantry. When Denise played cards in the church basement for the first time after the spirit communication, she said Kristina and the spirit in the pantry were still present. But what was the affect of the spirit communication on me? Kristina now seemed so real to me that I stood by her display case when no one was nearby, and told her she didn't need to stay any longer, and should go to her mom and her other relatives who had passed over. I admit I was careful that no one was around to observe me talking to her. But later, I would see other people, in turn, standing alone by the display case and talking to Kristina. Our skepticism had been shaken!

6 Kristina

Kristina had been no more to those of us at the historical society than just a name given to the old church in her memory. Now, incredibly, she/her ghost seemed totally real and alive, and I think we all felt a sense of horror to think of her nightmarish entrapment in the church. One woman at the spirit communication told us that she would certainly hate to think of one of her own kids being trapped like Kristina, and this seemed to be the general feeling of the group.

When Kristina was a little girl, she was very thoughtful and very active. When she was only twenty months old, she put out her hands to steady her younger sister's first attempts at walking. At Christmas, in later years, Kristina would have her dad cut down mistletoe with a long-handled saw, and she and her friends would mix it with pyracanthea berries and go around selling it to the neighbors for 50 cents a bundle.

Kristina loved to write. She wrote an imaginative essay for her class in school, telling how spiders came to have eight legs, and won the school creative writing contest. In fact she was an excellent all-around student in school. Her report cards are in the display cabinet, and they are all outstanding. She wrote plays and performed them with friends in an old building. She made paintings on pieces of wood, and then covered them with a layer of shellac.

Kristina became ill with leukemia at the age of nine and died at eleven. She had periods of remission from the disease when she could return to school. When she had to take time off from school because of the illness, the kids in her class would support her with visits and get-well cards. She was a strong little girl, who had great faith that her father could cure her. She would sit at the receptionist's desk in her dad's medical building, and tell people, "My daddy is going to make me well."

The impressions of her ghost that we heard from Tom, Denise, and Betty seemed to have many of the same characteristics she had as a little girl. Her ghost was filled with compassion for her dad and her unfortunate brother, loved her grandmother, was very active much of the time, and loved writing.

When Kristina died, her dad was holding her in his arms. He told her she was going to heaven. But, apparently, if we were to believe what we were being told, she did not go. Her spirit was in limbo in the old church. Why was this so? The doctor bought the old church a couple of years before her death, with the idea it would eventually be turned into a museum. After Kristina's death, the old church became a memorial to her and was named in her honor. Perhaps Kristina heard this and decided the church was where she should be, near her family who could not bear to lose her at such an early age.

In any case, Kristina's ghost began her terrible ordeal. Although she could try to play in her imagination with things that took her fancy in the church, this would prove to be a futile attempt to overcome the overwhelming sadness of her long imprisonment. One can imagine the despair she must have felt during the endless succession of long, dark, chilly, and lonely nights in the church. When people came to visit the church during the daytime, especially members of her own family, the frustration of being unable to make them even realize she was there would be like living in a real-life nightmare.

If there were other ghosts trapped in the church with Kristina, one could not expect them to be of much solace or help to her, since they would be caught up in their own overpowering feelings of sadness and hopelessness. Denise, being unusually sensitive to the emotions of spirits, avoided going into the pantry because the feelings of sadness she picked up were so strong that she had a feeling of depression even after she returned home from playing cards.

When Kristina's ghost first discovered that Betty, who was coming into the old church on a regular basis, was able to sense her presence, she must have been terribly excited. She would have thought that here was finally someone who could communicate with her and help her. The disappointment that came when Betty rebuffed Kristina's attempt for help must have been overwhelming. She would have had her hopes raised a second time when she realized that Denise could also sense her presence, but once again experienced bitter disappointment when Denise reacted with horror rather than understanding. The awful cycle of high hopes followed by great disappointment would have happened a third time when Tom came for his initial investigation and finally again when he arrived for the spirit communication, but was unable to free Kristina from the church. I was still not sure I believed in ghosts, but if there were such things, and if Kristina's was trapped in this old church, I was certainly going to do what I could to help her escape. I would do what I could to goad Tom into a more serious effort.

I must admit that this was not all altruism. I was becoming ever more interested in whether there were such things as ghosts. My brother has a friend who won great acclaim as an electrical engineering professor. Over time, however, his interests turned to more social questions and he became a futurist. While attempting to help clients (mostly commercial companies) predict the future he came up with an interesting theory. He came to believe that any phenomena reliably reported for three thousand years or more will eventually be verified by science. This has led him to the study of para-psychological phenomena. Certainly ghosts have been reported for a very long time. This is more fun than soil science.

7   A Birthday and a Book about Abe Lincoln

I contacted Tom again toward the end of July 1997 and told him we wanted to take him up on his offer to come for more investigation of our ghosts. We scheduled a meeting to be held on Monday, July 28, 1997. However, on Monday afternoon Tom called and said he had been ill and still wasn't feeling well enough to perform at his best. We arranged instead to meet on Thursday, July 31, 1997. Tom, Jan, Judi Kuykendall, Elizabeth, and I were at the meeting on the 31st. Some of the others who were at the first spirit communication could not come either because they were out of town or because they were taking their summer vacations. Others undoubtedly either had lost interest or did not see this as their problem.

Before the spirit communication sitting began, Tom said he heard a hissing sound in the direction of Kristina's display case, and he asked us if we heard the sound too. I had not. He walked over to the area of the sound, and suddenly had a look of complete astonishment on his face. He said he felt an unseen, warm little hand grasp his hand, and he was led over to Kristina's display case, where Kristina pointed at a book about Abraham Lincoln (it was one of several books standing on end in a row), and said, "Tell daddy!" She said, "Daddy knows"---something he knows about the Lincoln book. We would later learn this was Kristina's favorite book. The doctor had taken Kristina and the rest of his family to historical sites in Washington DC and Philadelphia, and she was enthralled by the Lincoln Monument. She was so fascinated by these educational trips that she voluntarily wrote essays about them, with particular emphasis on Lincoln.

When we stood by the display case, Tom heard the hissing sound again. He asked if we heard it. I had not, but Elizabeth said she heard it. Tom and Elizabeth both said it sounded like breath being drawn in or out. Elizabeth said it was a soft sound, but since I was standing beside her, I should have heard it too. The four of us then held a spirit communication around an old wooden table, while Judi wrote notes at an adjacent table. Tom reported that Kristina said to tell her dad that it was time for her to go. Tom said she was afraid of her dad's reaction to her wish to leave, and needed permission from him.

43

He also said he heard a squealing high-pitched noise, but none of the rest of us heard it.

He further stated that her dad's wishing probably held her here. He said, "She is locked in by an energy field that allows her only to go to a certain point, and prevents her from leaving." When I asked Tom later what sort of energy he was talking about, he said he had used the word, energy, to give the idea that a force was holding her, but it was of some unknown nature and not electromagnetic energy. He said her dad's wishes empowered intelligences that had never been human, and they were also binding her here. Tom's statement that Kristina is bound by intelligences that are not human sounds very strange. I didn't bother to question him further because I was certain Tom would say things are very different on the other side, as he has told us various times. He is not trained as a scientist and tends to use terms like energy and force rather wildly. However, it wasn't scientific rigor that we were interested in at this point.

Tom went on to say that Kristina believes her grandmother has the ability to appear to the doctor in his sleep and influence him in ways that will allow her release. The sign this is happening would perhaps appear when he removed some of the artifacts from Kristina's display. Tom's theory was that the binding was rooted in the doctor's sense of responsibility. He has a very strong sense of guilt over her death. He was a doctor and could not save his own daughter. Kristina was a very sensitive, loving girl, and doesn't want him to feel this. She wanted to be there to sooth him. She said, "If he knew that it didn't hurt, it would help him." But she desperately wanted to move on for her own development, and thinks her father needed to release her to move on in his life.

Tom said he heard Kristina say, "Tell daddy about the man who saw the girl there." This must have referred to his seeing Kristina looking out the window at him when he first came to investigate the old church. Tom's wife, Jan, then said she felt a cool breeze, as though a cold breath was in her face. Tom said, "Kristina is going to leave. She is very tired." Judi felt the cool breeze across her neck, as if Kristina was passing by.

Jan then asked, "Kristina, what can I do to help you out?" Tom reported Kristina as saying, "Tell the creek people to go." I had no idea what this meant. The spirit communication then came to an end. We were all even more worried about Kristina. Jan had mentioned that she had driven by the church on her way to work during the previous day. During the session Tom had asked Kristina if she tried to speak with Jan when she was driving by, as he said he saw an image of Kristina running out beside the street to flag Jan down. Jan later said she had seen Kristina in the windows of the church tower, looking as if she was asking to get out. But Tom assured us that Kristina was not being harmed, just being held. He added that he ended the session because she was tired, and needed to stop communicating with us

After the sitting, we all walked over to Kristina's display case to look at the book about Lincoln. Tom noticed a card with "Leo" printed on it in the cabinet, and assumed this must have been Kristina's astrological birth sign. Elizabeth located a card with Kristina's name printed on it, and the date of her birth was shown as July 31, 1955. Our spirit communication session had been held on what would have been Kristina's 42nd birthday! We all sang happy birthday to her. We were amazed to find ourselves there on her birthday. I later learned Kristina's dad was also born on July 31. Tom later told me that he had not been sick on July 28th although he used that as an excuse when he said he could not come that day. He said he just had a feeling that he really didn't want to be there, and so he delayed the meeting for three days. He thought Kristina had caused these emotions so the spirit communication would be rescheduled on her birthday.

Tom next followed our request to examine the storeroom in the church basement. This storeroom gives Denise a feeling of horror and she refuses to enter it. Tom mentioned during his first visit that this location gave him the worst feeling of any place in the church. He wasn't aware of Denise's reaction to the storeroom at the time. After spending a few minutes in this location, he said something very bad happened in the storeroom, and perhaps on several different occasions. He would have to work upon it at a later date. Upon leaving us, he concluded our meeting by again apologizing for not being able to free Kristina from the church. He said he did all he could do, and some other means than a spirit communication would be needed to resolve the situation.

We then discussed Tom's telling us that Kristina wanted her dad told about the Lincoln book, and about Tom's seeing Kristina looking out a church window at him. He had said Kristina thought this would get a conversation started that could lead to his finding out she was trapped in the old church and needed his permission to leave. Connie, who had been on vacation at the time of the second spirit communication, volunteered to talk to the doctor about these things. None of the rest of us had the nerve to volunteer to do this for fear of upsetting the doctor. We were delighted that the very attractive and kind-hearted Connie would volunteer to do so because she was obviously the best person to discuss these issues with him. She even resembles the doctor's late wife, and he is very fond of her.

She decided to talk to the doctor in the church basement, where we had the two spirit communication sittings, and near to Kristina's display case. She made arrangements to meet the doctor there on Saturday, August 30, 1997, not telling him the true purpose of the meeting

8   The Unmaking of a Skeptic

Some of us who spent a lot of time in the church developed the habit of speaking to Kristina when we passed her display case on the way up the stairs from the basement. We weren't sure if she was listening, but we would typically at least say, "Hi Kristina!" On Saturday, August 23, 1997, I stopped by the display case and explained that Connie would be talking to her dad on the following Saturday, and, hopefully, this would allow her to be released from the church. Then Jean and I went on up the stairway to see that all the doors were closed in the old church so we could activate the burglar alarm.

I was on the stage in front of the pews, and Jean was in the adjacent hallway with the door closed between us, when I was startled by the voice of a girl coming from the direction of the pews. The voice sounded excited and happy, and it spoke for a few seconds before stopping. I could not make out the words. I did not hear the voice again after the initial burst of talking.

It was definitely not Jean's voice. It came from another direction than Jean's location, and it was not muffled, as Jean's voice would have been with the door closed between us. I am sure the voice could not have come from outside, since only yells can be heard coming from outside, and this voice was speaking in normal tones. I was over fifty feet from the wall and stained glass windows that are behind the pews when I heard the voice. When someone with excellent hearing later stood on the same spot where I had been, and listened for my voice as I spoke outside the church in loud conversational tones (as one would use when speaking to someone with very poor hearing), they couldn't hear any sound at all.

The next day I was telling my mother and my aunt about this strange experience. My mother had been ridiculing our ghost stories from the beginning as she thought the idea of ghosts was total foolishness. She would say we were letting our imaginations run away from us, and the whole thing was just nonsense.

I was to be very surprised when I heard her reply to my story. It turns out she had her own ghostly experience at about the time of our first spirit communication (which she didn't attend), and had not intended to tell me about it, but it just slipped out as she and my aunt and I were talking. She had been working in what we call our stone house, which is an old building adjacent to the path leading to our front porch. She said that she had heard footsteps approaching the stone house on the series of concrete slabs that make up the path. She said the footsteps were light, sounding like a child wearing sandals or light shoes, and that the sound of the walking made her think these were the steps of a little girl rather than a boy. She said boys walk with a clunk, clunk, clunk sound, whereas little girls hurry along with quick little steps.

The sound of the footsteps went by the screen door at the front of the stone house, and continued up onto our front porch. My mother assumed she would hear a knock at the door, but she did not. She stepped out of the stone house to see who was on our front porch, and was astonished to see nobody was there. She looked around the yard, looked inside our house, and even knocked on the door of the rental house next door to see if anyone was there. There was no one anywhere.

She was very puzzled, since she assumed a child had walked by. As you probably remember, in one of our spirit communication sessions, Tom had reported that Kristina was trying to communicate with me because we both liked to write. He thought she might try to express herself through my writing. Since I only write at home, and never at the historical society, Tom suggested that Kristina might come home with me at times. This incident made me think about some other strange things I had experienced at home. I wrote about them in my notebook, but I had previously discounted them, since I assumed Kristina was always trapped in the church.

After I returned home from our first spirit communication in April 1997, I was writing down my recollections of incidents that occurred during the session. I wrote the following lines in my notebook: "Tom said she wants to write. Likes to write in color with crayons or colored pencil. We may find some writings." As I wrote these lines, I smelled a delectable, sweet-scented fragrance that seemed sort of natural and familiar. I recalled that Tom said a very pleasant, sweet-smelling odor may be a sign of a ghost, if no natural source of the odor can be located. The odor lasted only a very short time, and I could find no possible source of it. Was it Kristina reacting to what she saw me writing in my notebook?

Another incident occurred on August 15, 1997, just about a week before I heard the girl's voice in the church. I was at home thinking about various things while lying on the bed in my back room, where I do my typing on a computer. I heard the sound of a girl's voice nearby. The sound of the voice lasted only a short time, like the voice I heard a week later. The voice I was to hear in the church on August 23 also sounded similar to the voice I heard in my bedroom on August 15. I could not make out the words in either case.

The window of the room was open, so I thought the voice might have come from outside. When I went outside to look, I didn't see anyone around. Since I live in an orange grove, it is quite a distance to the nearest homes, and the sound was too close to have come from there.

9   Connie Shows her Courage

On Saturday, August 30, 1998, Connie had a talk with the doctor in the basement of the church. She planned to tell him about some of the evidence that Kristina's spirit was still spending time in the church, and to let him know about Tom's conclusions that Kristina wanted permission from her father to leave. We were nervous about this conversation because we didn't know how he would react to what Connie would tell him.

Connie wisely refrained from using such words as ghost or haunting, and told him a few stories that hopefully would show Kristina as an intelligent and caring entity. Connie told the doctor about Betty and Denise independently coming to the conclusion there was the spirit of a girl in the church, and about Denise's anguished reactions to Kristina's apparent desire for help at the time of her brother's death and when the doctor came to arrange and clean the items in the display case. As Connie told about these reactions of Denise to the ghost, the doctor volunteered the suggestion that extra-sensory perception might be involved.

Connie then told him that she had arranged for Tom Hagman to come and investigate the case. She did not say I invited Tom, because she didn't want to implicate any of the Rialto Historical Society's board members in these activities in case the doctor would become very upset about what had happened (I am on the board but Connie is not). She told the doctor about Tom's report that, when he arrived, he saw a girl looking at him out of the church window who appeared to be about eleven- or twelve-years-old. Connie also told him Tom's conclusion that the girl was there because she was so concerned about her father, and she needed her father's permission to leave. Connie said the doctor listened attentively. If he thought she was crazy, he never let a hint of it show.

The doctor then told Connie that he had held Kristina in his arms while she died, and that Kristina knew that she was going to heaven. Connie replied that she was sure Kristina had gone to heaven, but she suggested Kristina might have come back to look out for her father after he moved her ashes from a mausoleum in San Bernardino to the display case in the church. Also, she might have thought he needed her help because he had become isolated from members of his family, who had moved off to other locations. Connie said she got the doctor to say it was all right for Kristina to go. He said this a couple of times during their talk. She said she was not sure his heart was in it, however.

To our relief, and perhaps surprise, Kristina's father did not seem uncomfortable with supernatural phenomena. He told Connie he had a near-death experience when he was in Vietnam. He did not tell her what nearly caused him to die, but said he heard himself pronounced dead by a doctor who was also a nun. He saw an incredibly beautiful light, and could barely keep himself from going to it.

Before Connie and the doctor started their conversation, Elizabeth gave him a large envelope containing letters written by third graders from a local elementary school who were expressing appreciation for a tour of the Rialto Historical Society. The letters also told what had most impressed them during their visit. Many of them mentioned Kristina and the display case of her possessions, and about six of the letters showed drawings of the church with a girl (undoubtedly Kristina) looking out a window of the church. Connie said, "Look, this is just what Tom reported seeing. Maybe little kids have an ability to sense things that most of us lose when we get older."

Several times when the conversation began to wander to other topics, Connie took the discussion back to Tom's conclusions that Kristina needed permission to leave, so the doctor would be sure to get the point. Each time she brought this up, she would say, "I hope that you will not be offended if I say this." The doctor told Connie how much Kristina liked to write (just as Tom had said), and pointed out in the display case the story about spiders Kristina had written. When Connie asked the doctor about the Lincoln book (as noted earlier, Tom said Kristina wanted this mentioned to her dad), the doctor said this was Kristina's favorite book. Connie was amazed, as the rest of us were later when she related this answer to us.

The doctor told what a loving girl Kristina had been (just as Tom said during the spirit communication sittings). He also said that his oldest daughter, who is now deceased, experienced such extraordinary dreams about Kristina that she had called the doctor on the phone from her home in Arkansas to tell him about them. The dreams were so lifelike they seemed real to her

Connie told the doctor that other people also had extraordinary experiences in the church relating to Kristina. She told him I kept a log of all these events, and let him know he could get a typed copy from me if he would like to see it. When I told Tom about Connie's discussion with the doctor, Tom said, "We'll see what happens when things have time to settle." Tom thought the doctor might ask me for a copy of my report within a few weeks after Connie's talk with him, but he never asked to see it. Also, he never mentioned to me, or, as far as I know, to anyone else that Connie told him Kristina's spirit was in the church.

During a phone conversation I had with the doctor after his talk with Connie, he sounded very happy. He asked if Connie was a board member of the historical society, and, when I said she was not, he said she should be. He said she was a very hard worker, a great organizer, and a terrific person. He praised her lavishly and at great length. I can't imagine he would have recommended her for the board (she would be a great board member, but doesn't have the time to serve) or praised her so strongly if he thought her ideas about Kristina's presence and Kristina's need for his permission to go were total nonsense. He has always liked Connie, but he never recommended her for the board, and never praised her so enthusiastically until she told him the stories about Kristina.

Denise played cards with the group in the church basement in the middle of September for the first time since the second spirit communication, and for the first time since Connie talked to the doctor. Elizabeth asked her, "Is Kristina still here?" Denise said Kristina was still there and was very upset. Elizabeth hadn't told Denise anything about Connie's talk with the doctor before asking this question. Denise added that Kristina wanted to go and wanted someone to release her.

Elizabeth explained to Denise that Connie told the doctor about Kristina being in the church, told the doctor Kristina needed his permission to go, and said the doctor replied, "It's okay for her to go," a couple of different times during the conversation. Denise was surprised to hear this, and said, "Then she needs somebody else to release her." Denise suggested that Elizabeth try to release her.

Gerry, one of the card players, who had been a very close friend of Kristina's mother, heard the conversation and added some more information. She said Kristina's mother had become dangerously ill at some time after Kristina's death, and had a near-death experience of the type where people report leaving their bodies and moving toward a brilliant light. After Kristina died, her dad volunteered to go to Vietnam where he served as a doctor.

Denise had more bad vibrations the next week when the doctor came to clean Kristina's display case while she was again playing cards in the basement of the church. When he first began to work on the display case, Denise became extremely hot. As he continued to work, she began to feel very chilly, and she said her nose felt especially cold. Elizabeth said the church basement did not feel at all cold to her on this hot summer day. Denise left the church basement for a time to escape the feeling of cold, although Elizabeth said the area where Denise found relief in the main museum building to the north of the church felt no warmer to Elizabeth than the church basement.

Denise told Elizabeth that if she couldn't get over the horrible feelings she was picking up from Kristina, she might not be able to play cards in the church anymore. She said something had to be done. We all were distressed to hear Denise's conclusion that Kristina was still in the church, and Connie was extremely upset when I told her this news. We had looked forward to hearing she was gone after Connie's talk with the doctor. Now we began to think our attempts to release her might have done more harm than good, with our failures having taken away her hope and given her a much deeper feeling of despair.

I told Tom that Denise said Kristina was still in the church and was very upset. Tom said this didn't surprise him, but that we should continue our efforts to solve her problem. By this time he was obviously deeply involved in Kristina's fate. We set a time of 6 PM on Tuesday, September 23, 1997 to meet at the church so Tom could find out why Kristina had not gone on and why she was so upset.

10 You Are Going to See a Show Today!

The night before our third spirit communication session, I had a very strange dream. I went to bed after midnight, and awoke with a great start during the early morning hours. I imagined I heard a loud voice say, "You are going to see a show today!" It seemed so real I took my flashlight and looked outside to see if someone was out there. I know I did not dream that I looked outside my window, because my mother, who sleeps very lightly, had seen my flashlight moving around the house and thought I might be sleepwalking (not that one uses a flashlight when sleepwalking). When I woke up the next morning, I wondered if the dream meant that something spectacular was going to happen at the spirit communication that day.

When we met in the church basement for the third spirit communication session, Tom and his assistant, Judi, were there, but Tom's wife, Jan, was not able to come. Elizabeth, Jean, Gerry (the good friend of Kristina's mother), Denise, a woman named Peggy, and I were there. Connie was not able to come.

Denise again had a white streak painted on one of her cheeks, this time with small designs created with black markings in and around the white streak. When she arrived, she walked around outside the church, raising one arm up toward the church. Then she walked through the entrance and kitchen area of the church basement, making the same gestures. I told Connie about this later, and she said Denise was summoning her spirit guides, especially her Cherokee Indian ancestors. At the first spirit communication, Denise wore a Cherokee jacket and Cherokee jewelry, but this time she was wearing shorts and a T-shirt. When she sat down, she placed a small stone mounted on a base in front of her. The stone had a white line painted across it. She didn't explain what it was, but we assumed it was some Native American object used for supernatural purposes.

When Tom first arrived, he wasn't sure whether we would have a spirit communication or not. He asked me to summarize what had happened since our last spirit communication, and I told him about Denise saying that Kristina was still in the church and was more upset than ever. Denise then gave us her own impressions. She said Kristina was becoming extremely discouraged about her attempt to escape from the church, and also speculated that the doctor might not have believed what Connie told him about Kristina being in the church. Tom replied it was possible the doctor did believe what Connie said, and was thrilled about the idea of Kristina being in the church and being present when he, for instance, cleaned the display case.

Denise then told about a strange experience that happened during the previous week's card game. She had accompanied Elizabeth upstairs when she went to turn on the air conditioner. At the top of the stairs there is a golden, braided rope that stretches across the stairway, which Elizabeth detached at one end and moved out of the way so she and Denise could pass by. Denise said she had clearly seen Elizabeth detach and move another golden, braided rope from across the bottom of the stairway, adjacent to Kristina's display case, before she and Elizabeth started up the stairs. The peculiar thing is there is no rope that stretches across the bottom of the stairway. Denise concluded she had seen a symbolic image of Elizabeth removing a rope near Kristina's display case, thereby removing the binding forces that held Kristina in the church.

Tom then put forward the suggestion that Kristina needed those of us in the session to release her in addition to needing permission from her father. He said if any of us had a strong desire for her to stay, it could prevent her from going. I admitted that I enjoyed the ghost stories enormously and had not wanted to see her go, but now felt she should go. Gerry asked if Kristina could hear our conversation. Tom said she could, and this was the reason he wanted us to have this discussion.

Finally, Tom decided we would have a short spirit communication. The session began at 7:00 PM. We again all joined hands to form a ring and closed our eyes, except for Judi, who sat taking notes. Tom said we should protect ourselves by imagining that all of us, including Kristina, were surrounded by white light. Tom said each of us should think of the most spiritual experience that we ever had (I thought of Kristina), and raise our spiritual selves to higher levels of consciousness, vision, and emotion. We should be receptive to Kristina and her needs, and to her soul's development. We should assist her in feeling safe regarding the problem of her release. We should bring to her this white light of protection.

He reminded us of his feeling that Kristina was afraid that if she left, her dad would die. He said we must agree to look out for her father and help him in any way we can. Tom said just as he can't be responsible for all of us, or we can't be responsible for him, Kristina must realize she can't be responsible for her father. He asked us to help her see that she is the only one standing between herself and God, and getting in the way of reaching her higher self. When she appreciates this, then we must help to release her. We must coordinate our consciousness for her release, seeking alignment with that power that will assist her in moving toward her destiny. He told us that Kristina wanted her father to know it was all right---she understood what had been said. She said it was not necessary to tell it to her father. He would feel it and have that understanding.

Tom then said he was seeing a point that was expanding, and opening up for Kristina to move through and that we needed to help her move through the opening. He asked Kristina's grandmother to be on the other side to help her. I felt tremendous anxiety and suspense at this moment, as I desperately hoped that Kristina would leave. The tension in the room was palpable. Tom then told us that Kristina had gone through, and we must seal up the opening with energy. He said Kristina would know what to do. He said we should use our mind power, not our emotions, to seal up the hole.

At 7:10 PM the spirit communication ended. The first thing Tom said after the session was over was, "Who is Charles?" We all were puzzled by this remark. Then, Tom told us that a male spirit suddenly appeared after Kristina left, outside the entrance to the room in which we were seated, and said, "My name is Charles." Tom asked if we knew anyone named Charles who had been connected with the museum. Elizabeth remarked that Charles McLaughlin, who died in 1991, was one of the most important contributors to the Rialto Historical Society. He was a professional photographer who spent countless hours in the museum as a docent, and contributed most of the collection of historic Rialto photos, which he had taken himself as far back as the teen-years of the twentieth century. He was also a great source of information with his extraordinary memory and innumerable stories about early day Rialto. Could this be the man who was trapped in the pantry? Denise had also been startled when she sensed the spirit's appearance at the doorway, and she said he had never come out of the pantry before.

There were other people named Charles who had important connections with the church. Charles McLaughlin's father, also named Charles McLaughlin, played an important role in getting the church started. There was also a young minister in the early1920s, named Charles Sanders, who loved to sing and who sometimes delivered his entire sermon in song. There were undoubtedly others named Charles who had been associated with the church during its long history. A new mystery to entertain ourselves with at a later date.

Leaving the question of Charles for the time being, we began discussing our experiences from this spirit communication. Judi mentioned that while the hole for Kristina was opening up, Denise's arms went up, she began shaking, trembling and mumbling, and then audibly telling Kristina to go through. Her arms dropped after Kristina moved through the hole. Denise had no memory of doing any of these things. Denise said she saw an image (with her eyes closed) of a bright light in the direction Tom said Kristina took when she left. Elizabeth felt a touch on her knee at this same time. Tom said he saw someone waiting for Kristina on the other side of the hole---presumably Kristina's grandmother.

Gerry, who was sitting to my right and holding my right hand, said she felt a presence pass by her left side. She said it felt the same as when somebody walks by and stirs the air. I felt my right arm being pulled up and thought it was Gerry who was doing this. Judi was watching and never saw my arm move. Gerry also said she didn't feel my arm move. Tom explained that Kristina passed between Gerry and me when she left, and had raised my arm "psychically." Tom told this before either Gerry or I had a chance to relate our stories of sensing her passage by us.

Could someone have reached over and lifted my arm when my eyes were closed? I am certain nobody who was present would have done such a thing. In addition, everyone was holding hands; Tom was

15 feet away on the other side of the circle; Judi, Tom's assistant, was also on the other side of the room taking notes; and Gerry, whose word I absolutely trust, said she didn't feel my arm move.

Now that Tom had said Kristina was gone, the question that immediately came to all of our minds was whether both Tom and Denise would no longer be able to sense Kristina's presence in the church. Someone asked Denise if she felt Kristina was gone, and Denise answered that she could no longer feel Kristina's presence, but she was worried she might soon discover Kristina was still there. Tom also said he could no longer sense Kristina was there. Denise and Tom walked to the base of the stairway and moved close to Kristina's display case, where both had always felt her presence so strongly. They both said they no longer experienced the familiar feelings that Kristina's nearness brought.

Denise was ecstatic. She said she would be able to enjoy this feeling from now on, and she would simply ignore the ghost in the pantry and the bad sensations the storage room gave to her. Denise said she always had a feeling that if Kristina left, the ghost in the pantry and the bad feelings she experienced in the storeroom would disappear at the same time. Unfortunately, as we shall see later, this was not to happen.

While we were all sitting and talking in the basement of the church after the spirit communication, a strange incident occurred which caused the woman named Peggy to think Denise had actually read her mind. Denise and Peggy were sitting silently beside one another, when Denise suddenly said to Peggy, "Oh, you don't need to worry about that." This startled Peggy because she had not been talking to Denise. Peggy said Denise looked startled too, then became apologetic for making the remark and looked like she felt bad that she had revealed herself as being able to read Peggy's mind.

Peggy, at first, wasn't sure what she might have been thinking that had caused Denise to make this reply. She then recalled that she was thinking about what Tom said about the spirit world, and the thought passed through her head, "What about evil spirits?" She figured this was the only really negative thing in her thoughts Denise could have responded to. When Peggy asked Denise if this was what she was replying to, Denise didn't say anything, but nodded her head knowingly. I asked Denise if she read Peggy's mind, and she said it happened because there was "so much energy." A little later, when everyone was outside in the parking lot preparing to leave, Denise said to Peggy, "There are evil spirits but you don't have to worry about that." When I was talking with Denise, months later, she told me she sometimes picks up people's thoughts.

We were all delighted to think Kristina had left. It was a tremendously thrilling evening, and when I called Connie at her home to tell her Kristina was gone, she shouted with joy. When Denise next came to play cards in the old church, however, we couldn't help but worry that Denise might again sense Kristina's presence in the church. I was not present when Denise next came to play cards, but Elizabeth and Jean were and they both told me what happened. Elizabeth said she never saw Denise so happy. She joyfully went up the stairs and into the sanctuary, both locations that had caused her such dread when Kristina was in the church that she avoided them. Denise said it was wonderful to sense Kristina was gone, and to know she was with her grandmother. Denise had never been so happy to be in the church. She went upstairs into the sanctuary with a big smile on her face.

Denise has never felt Kristina's presence during the many times she has played cards in the church since our third spirit communication, and Tom and Jan both said they could no longer sense her presence when they returned to the church.

11   A Ghost Portal

If Kristina was truly gone, as Tom, Jan, and Denise claimed, who were the ghosts, if any, that remained in the old church? Several people concluded there was a ghost in the pantry, and the two different pairs of policemen answering the burglar alarm years apart saw the ghost of a middle-aged woman in a Victorian dress. Betty, the psychic card player who first reported Kristina's presence, sensed not only a ghost in the pantry, but also the ghost of a woman in her 50s or 60s who approached her in the church's kitchen. She also told of other ghosts that were in the church basement on one occasion just before people arrived to play cards. Were these ghosts still here, or had some or all of them merely been figments of people's imaginations?

The next investigation of the historical society's ghosts occurred, appropriately, on Halloween night of 1997. Denise played cards in mid-October, and told Elizabeth the ghost in the pantry was confused, disoriented, and didn't know what it wanted. I called Tom and told him what Denise said about the ghost in the pantry. Tom asked, "Shall we clean out the church?" I said that sounded like a good idea and he suggested we hold a spirit communication on Halloween night. He said, "We will have a great party!"

Halloween is now a time for dressing up in costumes and trick or treating, but it was a day of great importance in ancient times. During the Celtic festival of Samhain, which marked the start of the Celtic year, huge fires were lit across the countryside to scare away evil spirits and guide the spirits of the dead to revisit their homes. Halloween (hallowed or holy evening) was a festival in Medieval times, observed on October 31, the eve of All Saints' Day. The two merged over time into the present tradition, with the tales and customs connected with ghosts and witches coming from the Celtic festival.

Who were the Celtics? They were groups of people who took over political and cultural leadership in Central and Western Europe, including Britain, between 1200 and 400 BC. Their pre-Christian religious leaders in ancient Britain, Ireland, and Gaul were called the Druids. The Druids may have had their good points, but they were also a scary bunch who conducted human sacrifices by shooting their victims with arrows, impaling them on stakes, stabbing them, slitting their throats over cauldrons (and then drinking the blood), or burning them alive in huge wickerwork cages. The Celtic heyday ended with their defeat by the Romans in the first century AD.

The Celts believed the spirits of the dead could easily enter the world of the living on the evening of October 31, and we were about to see if the spirits of the dead could also easily be banished from the living world on that evening.

Denise did not want to come to the Halloween meeting because she did not like the idea of holding it on that night, and also because she knew that being near the ghost in the pantry would give her bad feelings. She did not think it was necessary for her to be there, since the ghost in the pantry had never sought her help, as Kristina had, and since she felt Tom was so capable he would not need her help.

When we met for the spirit communication, Tom, Jan, Judi, Jean, Elizabeth, Peggy, and I were present. Tom informed us that the man in the pantry couldn't go through the door into the main room of the church basement---he was stuck in the pantry area. Shortly afterward we heard a creaking noise that seemed to come from the floor near where Jan was seated, and Tom said, "He is here. We can get started." We were wondering if the ghost would turn out to be our old friend Charles McLaughlin, but we were about to get a big surprise.

Tom said he saw a man in a T-shirt with a big 1 printed on the front. He said the printing was fluorescent green as though it was being viewed under black light. The ghost was wearing a Levi jacket and was very dirty. Tom asked who he was and what he was doing there. The man replied that he was Charley's friend and said, "We don't have anyplace else to go." Tom said later that he didn't think Charles regarded this man as a friend. We expected only one ghost in the pantry, but Tom said there were several ghosts in the room. He said they were dirty and unkempt like homeless people, and they arrived and left through an invisible portal in the kitchen area. He said they sought help from Charles, but Charles wanted to keep them out of the church. Tom saw the ghost of a stout, but not overly fat, gray-haired woman with a Germanic look who also wanted to keep the homeless ones out of the church.

It seemed ridiculous to hear of so many different ghosts being reported in the church, because we have no records of anyone being murdered or even dying there, and one would think that deceased members of the congregation should have moved on to heaven rather than hanging around the church. There are many stories about the existence of ghost "portals" that allow ghosts to arrive easily from elsewhere. They have been claimed to exist in some cemeteries and buildings, and tales of gatherings of dozens and even hundreds of ghosts have been told. Native Americans reportedly built their burial grounds near such portals so the spirits could travel back and forth between the worlds of the living and the dead. Could such a "doorway" allow ghosts to come from other places to seek help or refuge in our church? To our mixed interest and consternation, Tom pointed out to us exactly where he detected an invisible doorway of this type. Later in this book, I will tell of a couple of other people who came to the church without being told about the presence or location of this portal and independently recognized it and described it as being in precisely the same location where Tom claimed it to be.

Tom said he could actually see the barriers that trap some ghosts. He said these are energy fields that serve as boundaries between different dimensions. He told us that they look like honeycombs to him, with individual cells that trap ghosts, and said that these cells are sometimes very large. He said a portal is a hole in an energy field, and he does not know what causes it. We were reminded that Tom had told of seeing a hole opening through which Kristina's ghost had passed the moment she was released from her entrapment in the church during our previous spirit communication session.

Tom said the ghost of the gray-haired woman in the church kitchen was trying to seal up the portal with a strip of metal. He suggested we try to seal up the portal using our minds to focus the white light like a laser beam. We tried, but we probably lacked a bit of commitment and confidence. Even though our group was at this point much under Tom's spell, we became somewhat reluctant at this point. The case of Kristina's ghost seemed relatively reasonable, giving the presence of her ashes and the items in the display case and the relationship between the church and her father. But this was stretching it a bit for us. We were already thinking that people would think we were crazy if they knew we believed there were hobo ghosts in the pantry. If they suspected our sanity after hearing us tell of the filthy ghosts, they would probably be convinced beyond the shadow of a doubt that we had lost all of our senses if they heard that we tried to seal up an invisible portal by using our minds like lasers.

But the session was definitely not lacking in excitement. For instance, early on Jan heard a woman's screams coming from the nearby storeroom, but she wasn't sure whether the woman's ghost was actually there or whether she was sensing the memory of an event, an occasional confusion that plagued her. I smelled some extremely foul odors, and then heard Tom say he smelled a terrible stench, although he couldn't remember smelling the odors afterward. Others also recalled that Tom mentioned smelling a foul odor during the spirit communication. I assumed the odors I smelled must have come from the trash. Later, I learned there was no trash in the trash can, and only Tom and I smelled foul odors. Tom said a horrible odor is often one of the signs a ghost is present. He told us that the odor often smells like sewage, and if you can't locate a natural source of the odor, you might have a ghost. He said the presence of a spirit might also result in the scent of flowers or some other pleasant odor.

A skeptic might say the odor was due to someone's flatulence and the others present were simply too polite to acknowledge it. The odor I smelled was an even fouler odor than the hydrogen sulfide resulting from flatulence, and the others present were certainly not too polite to have mentioned their recollection of any odor to me afterward. Since we were all sitting close together, it seems impossible the other people would not have smelled the odor, since they all have a very good sense of smell and most of them are very finicky about bad odors. A man who was a very highly motivated researcher on local history, but who stank to high heaven because of his aversion to bathing, used to come into our museum, and Elizabeth and Jean would complain about this in the strongest terms after he had left. I can't imagine that they would have noticed that man's body odor with such distaste and failed to notice the much fouler odor I smelled during the spirit communication.

Incidentally, after this session I recalled that there have been a couple of times in the past that unaccountable odors had been detected in the pantry. After our earlier spirit communication in which Tom announced that Kristina had been released, he went into the pantry and noticed an odor that smelled like decay. We all crowded in to see if we could smell the odor too, but no one else did. Tom said someone might have died in the pantry, although we have no information about whether that happened or not.

I noticed a strong and disagreeable odor that smelled like someone who had not taken a bath in months and mentioned this to the group. Everyone present at the spirit communication was neat and clean, so this was puzzling to me. No one else noticed this smell either, although it did not seem possible to me that they could have failed to smell it. The situation reminded me of the weird sounds during the first spirit communication that some could hear and others could not. Were the smells of a supernatural nature, so some people were sensitive to them but others were not?

About a month after the Halloween spirit communication, I was to briefly sense a strong, but not unpleasant, musty decay odor in the pantry. Denise said she often experienced such an odor when she went into the pantry, and sometimes she would even sense it when she was outside the pantry in the kitchen. Once, she told me she could smell it when I was in the pantry with her, but I could not smell a thing. Tom also told of experiencing a decay odor in the pantry. Could I have smelled the same odor Tom and Denise had sensed?

The musty, decay odor was not a normal smell of the pantry. Elizabeth and Jean had recently cleaned the pantry when I smelled the odor, and there was no garbage in the kitchen that might have wafted such fumes into the pantry. I had never smelled this odor, which matched so closely the description of the odor that Denise connected with the pantry, until this one brief period of a few seconds and was never to smell it again afterward.

After our Halloween spirit communication session had gone on for a half-hour or so, Tom said he had begun to feel tremendous heat, and he would have to end the sitting. When we discussed the session, he also said he had felt as though he was being pulled toward the invisible portal through which he said the ghosts entered and left the church. Elizabeth, who was sitting directly in front of the position where Tom claimed the portal to be located, said she felt comfortable during the spirit communication until near its end, when she felt so hot she thought she would have to remove her jacket. After the session ended, she felt comfortable again. She then spoke about the homeless people who come to the church to sleep under the bushes or to ask for food. Tom said the homeless people might attract similar spirits of the dead.

Judi said that during the last part of the spirit communication, when we were trying to seal the portal, she felt very nauseous. She said this was odd because she almost never feels nauseous.

Tom added that he felt as though a weight had become progressively heavier on him during the spirit communication, and when he ended the session the weight lifted and he felt much better. He walked around the pantry, kitchen, and storage room areas, and said that what he experienced before as an oppressive feeling, now didn't feel so bad. He asked Jan for her impressions, and she felt that something still had not been resolved. Tom said we would have to wait and see what happened.

After the spirit communication was over, we were anxious to see what effects it might have had on our ghosts, so I asked Denise if she could come to see what her impressions were (she had not been at this spirit communication). The Halloween spirit communication had been on a Friday, and Denise stopped by the following Wednesday to see what she could sense. As she walked into the pantry, she shivered two or three times, even though it did not feel cold to me. She said she smelled a musty odor of decay, which she often noticed in the pantry, but which I could not smell that day. She went on to say that the pantry felt different to her than it ever felt before, but she still sensed that spirits were there. At first, she thought her feelings may have come from energy left over from the recent spirit communication, but then she concluded there were still ghosts in the room. She said the pantry felt "busier" to her, as though the ghosts had been stirred up.

Denise said that previously she would pick up a terrible feeling of depression every time she went into the pantry, but now, for the first time, she could go into the pantry without experiencing this. As time passed after the Halloween spirit communication, she only occasionally would have a feeling that something was still in the pantry. She had the impression that Charles, who had given her such a strong feeling of depression, and perhaps other spirits from the pantry had left the church.

12 Who's Still Here?

I was anxious to have Tom return to the church and see what he would sense a few months after the Halloween spirit communication. Would he feel the building was still haunted or would he conclude the ghosts were all gone? I seemed to have moved from the leading skeptic in the historical society to leader of the campaign to understand what was going on. I had also come to know Tom better and gain increased respect for his motivations and his work. He was a truly dedicated man seeking the truth about spirits on his own time and money. I can tell you from first hand experience that it is much more difficult to study spirits than soil.

Tom had invited me to join his study and discussion group that meets once a month, and I accepted, because once again I thought it would be interesting – amazing how interest can lead you in directions you might think you would never take. I found that many members of this study/discussion group considered themselves to be psychic, and I thought it would be fun to have the group hold one of their meetings in the old church and see what they would turn up. The group happily agreed to meet in the old church, and the topic of discussion for the evening would be surviving death. They were told no details about what had transpired before. We arranged for them to come on an evening in April 1998.

At the appointed time a couple of dozen people arrived in the church. Most were from Tom's group, but there were a few he did not recognize---undoubtedly friends of some of the others. Tom pointed out a couple of people to me who he said were very skeptical of the idea of ghosts. Denise did not come, and only Elizabeth and Jean and I were there from our historical society. Tom's group sat in the basement of the church as he began his opening remarks. He told them he would give them no details about ghosts that might be present or about ghostly events which had happened previously, but would allow them to roam freely through the building to see what they could sense. Then, everyone would gather again in the church basement, and those who observed something interesting would tell the group about it. He told them not to discuss their observations among themselves until we all met again after their investigations were finished. He concluded his opening remarks by showing us examples of equipment people have used to investigate ghosts, including the equipment he had brought on his original visit to the church and some additional items such as copper dowsing rods. He explained all the equipment to us but said he has found that his own psychic powers are much better than any apparatus when it comes to investigating ghosts.

The members of the group then spread out through the church and adjacent museum building, some carrying dowsing rods or pendulums. Each went along slowly, stopping at various locations to try to sense the presence of a ghost. I spent the time walking around and watching them at work. Many were obviously getting excited when they reached such areas as the pantry or the location by the piano in the church sanctuary where Tom and Denise had each experienced a cold spot. Most were following Tom's instructions not to discuss things with each other until we met again. A few, caught up in the excitement of the moment when they encountered something, would say to someone standing nearby, "Did you see that?"

After about 45 minutes, they gathered back in the church basement to listen to Tom, and then to tell of their own experiences. Tom had told me previously that while people who investigate ghosts may be sensitive to the presence of a spirit, most of them tend to be inaccurate when it comes to giving details about the ghost. For this reason, he said that when a group of people gather to investigate a haunting it is best to look for patterns in what the people report (such as various people independently sensing the presence of a ghost in a certain location). He added that one should not place great confidence in the accuracy of the details that each one gives about the ghost. Tom told me that when he investigates a haunted building, he arrives with a skeptic's point of view, and, in most cases, he finds there is nothing to it, and the "ghost stories" have come entirely from peoples' imaginations. He goes once to such buildings and never goes back. He said if he were to invite 100 people anxious to encounter a ghost to come and investigate a building, virtually all would say they had experienced a ghost, even if none was present. His purpose for inviting various people to come with him to investigate possible hauntings is to use it as a screening method to see who can accurately sense the presence of ghosts and who can not.

Before the people started telling about their experiences and impressions, Tom went through a list of things that may indicate the presence of a ghost. As before, he that said a common sign of a spirit is a cold spot, where the chilly feeling can't be attributed to a draft or nearness to a cold object. This may occur in the middle of a room and be surrounded by warmer air. Another sign of a possible ghost is a draft of air in a location that is completely shut up so no such movement of air should be possible. Tom told of being in a haunted house with a group of people where a current of air moved mysteriously around the people. A third sign is the presence of inexplicable lights. Tom gave an example from a haunted house where he was lounging on a sofa and saw two balls of light. He thought this might be a spirit trying to communicate. Another indication was movement of objects without anyone or any natural force around to move them. He told of times that he or Jan left a room and returned to find a chair had been moved. Tom said when something turns up missing and then mysteriously reappears that could also be a sign of a ghost.

Tom said a dramatic manifestation of a ghost occurs when it touches or grabs a person. He told of a case where he was giving a class in a haunted house, and a ghost grabbed a woman's arm. It was possible to see the indentation afterward. I was present when Tom and Jan investigated a haunted house in Redlands, California, and the woman who lived in the house said she had been pinched by the ghost of a man as she worked in her kitchen. She said, "It scared the hell out of me!" The most spectacular manifestation of a ghost, of course, occurs when it is seen as an apparition. Tom said the apparition might even be an animal.

Obviously, it would be very easy to overlook some hard-to-find, but natural, explanations for some of these previously mentioned signs of a ghost, and conclude that one's house was haunted. For instance, a foul odor could be produced by any number of plumbing problems.

Tom and I had decided to talk to the people individually. We could tell by their eagerness to talk that most of them had stories of encountering what they took to be a ghost or ghosts. Tom had assigned me the role of interviewing the individuals in the group to find what they had discovered. I asked those with stories to come, one at a time, to where I was seated and tell me what had happened. Some people left before I had a chance to record their experiences and I had to talk to them on the phone afterward to get the details. A few I never did talk to because I did not know their names or how to reach them, so I undoubtedly missed some of the stories. The stories I heard were all interesting, but I wound up with a feeling of confusion. How could I tell which stories were accurate and which were not? I then remembered Tom's advice to place more emphasis on looking for patterns rather than trying to evaluate the accuracy of every single particular that people told us.

I will go into more detail about these patterns in the next chapter. Tom's conclusion after listening to the varied accounts given by the people in this group was simply that there were still ghosts in the building. None of the people, including Tom and Jan, sensed the presence of Kristina, though. Their stories particularly centered on either the pantry or on the upstairs room from which Kristina was looking at Tom when he first arrived to investigate the old church. This room was now used by grooms to prepare for the weddings in the church. I will henceforth refer to it as the groom's room. The room just to the south of this is called, not surprisingly, the bride's room.

The greatest number of ghost "sightings" took place in the groom's room. Mary Barnes, a woman who Tom credits with real psychic ability, had a frightening experience in this room. After she came into the room, she saw a misty form rush past her into the hallway and then go down the steps that lead to the south end of the hallway. It was apparently a ghost that had followed another woman, who was standing near Mary, up the stairs on her way to the groom's room, where it had sat in a chair. When Mary entered the room the ghost jumped up and left, rushing past her. The other woman, who had also seen the ghost, said to Mary, "Let's follow it!" The terrified Mary replied, "Let's don't!" They felt the chill of a cold spot where they were standing. Mary said she experienced an unpleasant feeling in her solar plexus as the ghost passed by. Tom explained that ghosts often have a misty appearance when the spirit forms its image from ethereal matter. Having learned about his use of terms, I did not question him on the nature of ethereal matter.

Strange things had been happening in connection with the groom's room for years before Tom's group came to investigate the church. When the burglar alarm is set without the door to this room being locked, the door sometimes opens by itself in the middle of the night, which sets off the burglar alarm. For this reason, Elizabeth kept the door locked after she finished with weddings so that she did not have to go to the church at 2 AM or 3 AM to let the police in to investigate the cause of the alarm. She was encouraged to do this by her husband, who would drag himself out of bed and go with her because he didn't want her driving to the old church by herself in the middle of the night. Other people in charge of the weddings before Elizabeth took over that role also kept the door to the groom's room locked for the same reason.

When I began spending time in the church I examined this door to find out why it had to be locked before it would stay shut. Elizabeth had a theory that the vibrations of passing trucks or the shock of a small earthquake would cause the unlocked door to open and set off the alarm. I examined the door closely to see if her theory might explain how it could open by itself. I have never seen, heard, or felt the door vibrating even slightly at times when the heaviest concentrations of traffic are passing on the road in front of the church. Also, there have been no earthquakes at the times when the door has come open by itself. I have pushed hard on the door when it was latched, or grabbed the doorknob and shook it violently in a direction toward me and away from me without having the door come open. There are also three other doors in the main part of the church that come open by themselves after they have been securely latched and after the burglar alarm has been set. However, these other three doors do not set off the burglar alarm when they come open.

When Denise heard about Elizabeth's theory that vibration from passing trucks or shaking from a small earthquake caused the groom's room door to open, she said, "The ghosts are opening the door!" After Denise no longer felt Kristina's presence, and after the changes in the pantry allowed her to go in that room without feelings of dread, she would happily go anywhere in the church, with the exception of the groom's room or the storeroom north of the kitchen. Both of these rooms continued to make her feel very uneasy.

What did Tom sense in the old church that night? Tom said that he still had his familiar old spooky feelings in the pantry, in the storeroom, and in front of the stove, and he felt that the ghosts had not all gone. When I told Denise about all the ghost stories the people in Tom's group had told me, she said too many people had come and they told too many stories about too many ghosts to be believable. She thought they may have picked up impressions from the artifacts in the museum, which had belonged to so many people, and which were associated with very important events in their lives such as graduations, marriages, and so on. Denise also suggested that the ghosts who are actually in the church might exist in separate realities and may not even be aware of one another.

Tom suggested that all of our efforts to get Kristina and the other ghosts out of the church might have actually caused additional ghosts to come into the church. They might flock to where they believed they could get help moving on. He said Kristina might have been talking from the other side to the ghosts, and telling them, "If you go to the church, there's a man there who might free you." Tom said that ghosts would be able to enter the church through the portal that exists in the kitchen area.

I told Tom I was totally confused, and didn't know how I would ever make sense of what the people told me the evening his group visited. He suggested I could put on a program with another group to see if they came up with conclusions similar to those of his group. The next chapter will tell about someone who came to visit the church, and who, without having been told what Tom's group said, showed some extraordinary responses in the same locations where the group sensed ghostly activity.

13 Terror in The Church

On a gorgeous Saturday morning in September of 1998, my nephew, Bob, and his beautiful, blond girlfriend Julia drove out from Santa Monica for a visit. Julia is from England, and has a thrilling singing voice with a huge range. She composes her own music and has recorded her songs on five compact discs, which can be found for sale in any music store. She has a very large following of fans, tours all over the world to promote her recordings, and has supported herself by her singing nearly all of her adult life. She also has had some extraordinary psychic experiences. She saw her uncle's ghost after his death, had remarkable premonitions a couple of times (for example, getting a forewarning about the destructive 1994 Northridge, California earthquake), and has had incredible responses when using a pendulum for mystical purposes.

Because Julia told me about her supernatural experiences, I thought she might find it interesting to go to the old church and see if she could sense any ghosts. She enthusiastically accepted the invitation. I told her we could take the copper dowsing rods Tom had given me and see how they would work for her. She had never used dowsing rods. My nephew decided he would skip the trip to the church and use the time to visit with his grandmother.

The copper dowsing rods are supposed to move by themselves if you hold them in your hands and if you point them at a ghost. Tom said it is not clear whether the dowsing rods actually detect a ghost, or just energy. By now I knew Tom well enough to ask him what kind of energy he was talking about, and he knew me well enough to answer that he did not know. He uses terms common in physical science, such as "electromagnetic energy" to describe what he is sensing for want of a better term because he is not sure by what phenomena ghosts influence physical objects and communicate with people. He is a firm believer in the ability of a person with psychic abilities to locate ghosts and other objects with such rods. He does a demonstration with cups on a table to show which cups are empty and which are filled with water. Jan is also a believer in the combination of dowsing rods and sensitive people and says they are very useful for locating lost car keys and other objects.

About six inches of each of these rods is bent at a right angle, leaving about two feet for pointing. The dowser holds a rod in each hand, allowing the rod to balance on top of the forefinger. If the hands are held perfectly still and level, when the rods begin to move it feels as if they are being moved by some unseen, external force, and not by you.

Does the idea of dowsing for ghosts, or car keys, or water, or anything else sound completely crazy? Here, I must make a digression and talk about the dowsing rods before we get back to what happened to Julia in the church. Dowsing rods have of course been used for a long period of time for purposes such as searching for water. My grandfather dowsed for water long ago for our local water company using a dowsing rod made from fruit tree wood. He gave demonstrations to both my mother and my brother (my brother, a retired Stanford University professor of engineering, is ten years older than I am and has better recall of my grandfather, who died when I was only six). My mother and my brother both recall being very impressed when they felt the dowsing rod being pulled toward the earth by some unseen force. Since there are no physical explanations as to why a bent twig would point at the best location to drill a well, dowsing for water is no longer considered to be effective unless one happens to be dowsing over a large and shallow aquifer. Water companies tend to hire geologists instead of water witches. In the case of searching for ghosts, there is less controversy because people who might not believe that dowsing can locate ghosts generally don't even believe in ghosts.

I used the dowsing rods in the pantry and in the storeroom and was amazed to see them moving toward one another and then crossing over each other. Jean also tried them and the rods moved in her hands in both locations. We found no movement of the rods anywhere else in the church. The dowsing rods worked sometimes but not other times when pointed in various directions in the storeroom, and they worked on some occasions when pointed toward the back of the pantry. The rods would move when pointed in one direction, then stop, and then move again when pointed in another direction. This made it seem as though there were ghosts moving around and even ducking away from the dowsing rods. After the rods had been used for a short time in a room, they would stop moving in that location. Sometimes the ghosts seemed to be totally out of the rooms and the rods would not move at all on a given day.

Could I have inadvertently caused the dowsing rods to move by getting excited and unconsciously moving my hands when I was in the rooms where ghosts had been reported, whereas I held my hands still when I was in other places? I spent quite a lot of time wondering about this, but thought it less likely when I saw that the rods moved on some occasions but not at other times in the same location. I also would closely watch my hands and the rods at all times, and my hands were very still and level when I saw the rods moving. In addition, I repeatedly tried the rods in the groom's room, but they didn't move even though ghosts had often been reported in that room.

As months passed after Tom gave me the dowsing rods, the rods would move on fewer and fewer occasions in both the pantry and the storeroom. It was as though the ghosts were getting tired of all this nonsense and were moving out of the way before I could even start pointing the rods at them. Finally, the dowsing rods would refuse to move on nearly all of the days that I tried them.

The only place other than the pantry and the storeroom the rods had ever moved for me in the church was at the south end of the pew which is farthest toward the back of the sanctuary, and that was on only one occasion. This location was the exact spot that a woman who came with Tom's group described as the favorite sitting place of a nice ghost who brought ghostly flowers to the front of the church.

Now, let's return to Julia's visit to the church. I told her absolutely nothing about things that had happened in the various parts of the church, and I let her wander around the church with the dowsing rods to see what she would turn up. After we walked into the basement of the church, Julia said she sensed that something was coming down the stairs after us. Julia put her hands over her head, and said she had surrounded herself with the white light of protection. Obviously she was not new to this game. We went into the storeroom, where Tom and Denise always had such a feeling of horror, and I demonstrated the use of the dowsing rods to Julia. The rods did not move in my hands when I pointed them in various directions.

Julia then took the rods and tried pointing them in various directions in the storeroom. When she pointed them toward the north side of the storeroom, they moved toward one another until they crossed each other. When she pointed them toward the southeast side of the storeroom, they moved vigorously apart. Julia, who had never used dowsing rods before, was amazed. So was I. She said she must have been doing something with her hands that made the rods appear to move by themselves.

She next walked into the little hallway that leads into the storeroom and tried the rods again. The rods didn't move at all in the hallway. When she tried the rods in the kitchen, there was no movement, either. This made her think that she was not the cause of the rods moving. She then walked into the pantry and the rods moved apart from each other when aimed at the back of the pantry. When she stood in the pantry and aimed the rods toward the doorway at its front, the rods were perfectly still in her hands. She told me she didn't feel any fear, despite her amazement at seeing the dowsing rods move in both the storeroom and the pantry.

Now, Julia moved into the large basement room of the church and began trying the dowsing rods everywhere in the room. She went all along the walls and all over the middle of the room, and the rods did not move. She then pointed the rods at Kristina's display case at the bottom of the stairs (she didn't know the significance of this display case), and the dowsing rods moved apart. This surprised me because we all thought Kristina was gone. This must have been some leftover "energy" from Kristina.

My astonishment was complete. Julia's dowsing rods had unerringly found the locations in the church basement where ghostly activity had been reported by many people. When she pointed the rods at a large number of other locations in the church basement, they had not moved at all. I could hardly believe it. Julia had not been told anything about these locations and what people had sensed in them.

She was as accurate as if she had a Geiger counter and was locating scattered radioactive materials.

Next, we started up the stairs to see what we would find in the main part of the church. At the top of the stairs was a small broom closet, where many people in Tom's visiting group had said they experienced a bad feeling. Jan said she saw something in the closet that was not human and which looked like a gnome. Also, the door to this closet is one of the doors in the church that come open at times when we are sure nobody is in the church. Julia stuck the dowsing rods into the closet, and, just like clockwork, there was the movement again. She once again said she did not feel frightened by all of this, but that was about to change dramatically.

When we went into the church sanctuary, Julia pointed the rods at the wall behind the pews, and they each whipped around with incredible speed until they were pointing directly behind her at the area in the front of the pews. Julia said there was something drawing her there. We walked up onto the stage in front of the pews, and Julia started pointing the dowsing rods around the stage. Nearby was a small stained glass window with Kristina's name on it. Mary Barnes had tried dowsing rods by this window when Tom's group explored the church, and the rods had moved. Mary concluded that Kristina was gone but there was still energy present. Two other women had walked by the stained glass window, sensed a cold spot, and noticed that a pendulum carried by one of the women moved there. Denise had told me she sensed something bad by the window.

When we were near Kristina's window, Julia pointed the dowsing rods at it. The rods started moving violently. They flew outward so fast they bounced off her shoulders. Julia was holding her hands and arms still when the rods zoomed outward, and there was no way she could have caused their frenetic movement. We heard what sounded like a creak in the carpeted floor a few feet ahead of us, as if somebody had just stepped onto that spot and stood there. She was now clearly frightened. She felt that something was standing just in front of us, and I had the same feeling. Although she squeezed the dowsing rods so hard her knuckles turned white, she could not keep the rods from flying outward.

Next, Julia moved toward the piano on the stage. Both Tom and Denise had sensed a cold spot by the piano. Jan had said she felt an energy field by the piano, and she had the impression that one might go through there into another dimension. Inez had felt a cold spot by the piano when she came to the church with Tom's group.

When Julia reached the piano, the dowsing rods began to move fiercely once again. She now had a look of stark terror on her face and said she had a feeling of bitter cold pressing against her back and feelings of pain in her neck and back. It didn't feel cold to me by the piano.

We walked into the hallway behind the stage, and Julia started aiming the dowsing rods in various directions to see what they would show next. When she went into a short side hallway, which ran from the main hallway toward the stage, the rods flew outward until they hit against the sides of the doorway at the entrance to the short hallway. She told us that the rods were being pulled sideways with such force she couldn't pull them back in from the sides of the doorway until she struggled for a time. Nobody had ever said they sensed anything in this hallway, although the two doors that open from this hallway onto the stage have both come open in the empty church when they had been securely latched.

Our next stop was the notorious groom's room where so many people have experienced unsettling things. Julia went into the room and nothing happened for a second or two. Then the dowsing rods flew outward with the greatest force we were to see that day, bouncing violently off her shoulders. She was totally unable to control the rods. At the same time she reported feeling very weak as though something or someone was drawing energy from her. She said she felt as though she was about to faint. She later told me that she knew what it felt like to faint since she had once fainted when she was very ill. She said the room affected her more strongly than anyplace else she had been in the church, giving her a very heavy sad feeling. She suggested that we put a cross in the room and maybe burn sage there.

We left the groom's room and walked into the bride's room, just to its south. The only incident that had ever been reported here took place when Tom's group was exploring the church, and the two women in the bride's room thought that a spirit had passed by them. Julia kept pointing the rods in different directions in the bride's room and getting no response until she pointed the dowsing rods at a series of mirrors near the entrance to the room, and the rods moved.

The only other places in the church where a large number of people in Tom's group had sensed ghostly activity were in the balcony and in the bell tower above the balcony. I didn't have the special key to get into the balcony, Julia looked as if she had about all that she could take, and we needed to leave the church soon to meet others for lunch, so we did not go up to the balcony.

We stopped again by Kristina's window on the way out so I could perform a couple of tests. We stepped on the spot where we were standing when we heard the creaking noise coming from the floor ahead of us, but this time no creaking noise came from the spot in front of us. When I moved forward and stepped on the place where the creaking noise had originated, I heard the exact same creaking noise coming from below my feet. This made it seem that the creaking noise we heard before could not have been produced by our own feet on the floor. The rods were moving rapidly again in Julia's hands, and she said, "Have a happy life whoever you are!" Julia said she sensed mischievousness by the window. Could this have been the ghost of the boy that a woman who had come with Tom's group said liked to play tricks on Elizabeth and me? The woman had told me she sensed this ghost in the groom's room when Tom's group came to explore the church.

We left the church and walked over into the museum building. Julia tried the rods in different locations in the museum while I talked to some of the people who were working there. The only location the rods moved in the museum building was in a room with old clothes when they were pointed toward a chest and some turn-of-the-century ladies' dresses in the northeast corner. Betty, the psychic card player who was the first to say there was the ghost of a girl in the historical society, said Kristina liked to play with the clothes in this room.

I was stunned by Julia's experiences with the dowsing rods. In her hands the rods unerringly showed locations where ghostly activity had been reported, and they did not move in other places. It would not seem there was a ghost everywhere that the rods moved, but, instead, they may have picked up some sort of ghostly energy that remained in those locations. After we finished going through the church, I told Julia what had been reported in the places where the rods or her emotions had shown such strong reactions, and she was as amazed as I was.

As we were riding home, Julia said her exploration of the church was a fascinating experience, but she would never return there again. When we got home, she felt weak and faint. She said she never had such a feeling in her entire life. She wanted tea with her lunch, and afterward she felt so weak she had to lie down.

While she was resting, she continued to feel weak and her neck and back ached. This also alarmed her, since she never had pains in her neck and back. She had the terrifying feeling that something evil had attached itself to her back. She thought a ghost had become stuck to her when she was by the piano, and its bad effects on her became stronger as she went into the hallway, and especially into the groom's room. Then, she thought the ghost came home with her. After a little while, in a state of exhaustion, she fell asleep for two hours. When my nephew Bob went to check on her, she was awake again and still terrified. She told Bob she wanted him to ask me if it was possible for a ghost to become attached to a person's back. Bob came out of the room where Julia was resting and asked me about this. I was surprised by the question, but recalled that when I observed Tom investigating a haunted house in Redlands, California, a little over seven months earlier, this same subject came up.

He had detected a ghost attached to the back of the woman who lived in the house. She told him that before he arrived she had been lying down because of terrible neck pains. She had apparently suffered from frequent back and neck aches for many years, but thought this was caused by the stress of teaching high school classes. Tom had definitely not known this, but concluded that the ghost was causing her pain. After his session at the Redlands house, the ghost seemed to literally get off of her back. I called the couple periodically to see if they were continuing to have problems. Each time I called, I was told the woman was feeling great and her back and neck pains had disappeared. Whether the cure was psychosomatic, or whether the ghost was gone, or whatever else, she was ecstatic to have escaped from the terrible pain.

After Bob told Julia about Tom's diagnosis of the woman in Redlands, Julia asked Bob to say prayers by her neck and to brush her neck with his hand. She imagined a white light surrounding her, and also brushed behind her neck with her own hands. This seemed to make her feel better. Simultaneously she smelled a very foul odor, like sewage, for a brief instant in the room where she was resting. Bob did not notice this. She had heard that such an odor can be a sign of a ghost, and she thought a ghost might have been released from her back into our house. Julia did not tell me about this because she did not want me to worry that the ghost might be loose in the house.

When we had dinner that evening, Julia felt hot and tired but very hungry at the dinner table. After dinner she felt deeply tired and totally drained of energy. My mother had been astounded earlier in the day when she saw Julia go to the church full of energy and vitality and then saw her return looking totally exhausted after only an hour or so. I asked Julia if she would like to have the dowsing rods, and she said they were much too powerful and she would never touch them again.

After dinner, Bob and Julia left on their way back to Julia's house in Santa Monica. As they were leaving our driveway, Julia told Bob they should go back and tell us that a ghost might have been released in our house, but Bob said not to worry about it. He told her that if this had happened, the ghost would go back to the church. I later heard that after she returned to her home, Julia took a shower and did purifying exercises. The next day she took a salt bath in the ocean to further purify herself. That night, at a party for her friends, Julia told the group about her experiences in the old church. She said they all believed her except for one man who was totally skeptical about the idea of ghosts. The skeptic said I must have given her some unintentional clues by body language or some such thing when we reached the areas where ghosts had been reported. Julia assured him I had not, and I am also certain I did not do so. She was not even looking at me when she went to the different areas with the dowsing rods. The others all believed her because they had once seen an extraordinary case of one of her prophecies coming true.

The following day, Julia flew to London where she was preparing to do a promotional tour for a new compact disc of her songs. She still felt weak as if she had a cold or flu, but she didn't have either. There was something wrong with her throat, she could not talk, and she was afraid she would have to cancel her promotional tour. She was extremely upset because she never had voice troubles before and she depended on it for her livelihood and the pleasure she got from music and performing. A specialist examined her and told her that her neck muscles had swollen so badly they had cut off the blood supply to her vocal chords. He manipulated her neck, which seemed to help. She also told me that she has a psychic friend, Angie, who upon meeting her on her return sensed there was something wrong with her, although she knew nothing about her experiences in the old church. Apparently Angie saw what she described as a bundle of negative energy, grunted loudly and made a chopping motion with her hand across her neck. Julia immediately felt something had changed.

Despite all of this trauma, Julia was able to perform her concert tour, although her voice was still bad. The reviewer for the London Times didn't seem to mind the difference in the quality of her voice. He gave her a very good review and referred to her as a "husky angel."

I wondered if another ghost-sensitive person would have as strong a reaction with the dowsing rods as Julia did, and so I asked Denise to try them. She had been skeptical of dowsing rods, but they moved as violently in her hands as they had in Julia's. Despite trying so hard to hold the rods still that her thumbs became sore, the rods moved fiercely when she held them in the storeroom, in the pantry, and beside the piano. They also moved with great force in the hallway behind the piano, in the groom's room, and in various places around the church basement.

When I tried the rods, I had much weaker movement in a couple of places where she had powerful movement of the rods, and none at all in other places where the rods moved very strongly in her hands. Just as had happened when Julia used them, Denise's hands were perfectly still and level as the rods flew back and forth. Her hands or arms could not possibly have given such violent motion to the dowsing rods as I observed. Sometimes the rods would whip around so they were both pointing backward behind her neck, and at other times they would cross against her throat like they were going to choke her. Once when the rods had crossed against her throat, she said, "I know when I am not wanted!" As Denise walked around the church she said, "This whole place is loaded with things." She was exhausted when she went home after the session with the dowsing rods, and she said she slept like a log that night. The afternoon had showed me again that the response of the dowsing rods depended greatly on whom was holding them.

14   The Ghost in the Groom's Room

My experiences with ghosts in the church have almost always given me a feeling of fascination rather than fear. I felt the same reactions as if I had been watching rare wild animals from a place of safety, although my sense of amazement was far stronger than I could ever get from nature. Most of the times I felt real fear when dealing with spirits took place when I thought that a ghost was heading directly toward me. This occurred, for example, when Julia and I heard floorboards creaking in front of us in the church in such a way that it sounded like a ghost might be approaching. Although it didn't seem like a ghost would do anything bad to me, I still didn't like the idea that one had seen me and was coming toward me with some mysterious intent in mind. Maybe an evil spirit could kill someone by such means as pushing, tripping, or even distracting them so they would die in a fall on a stairway or elsewhere, or by turning their steering wheel to bring about a fatal collision. I asked Tom and Jan about this and they both said an evil spirit could kill someone.

I never felt the horror of ghosts that I saw mirrored on Denise's face or Julia's face when they met spirits in the church. I wondered why they experienced so much more fear than I did. Julia seemed quite brave to me, since she travels all over the world and sings in front of enormous crowds of people. Denise worries too much about too many things, and I thought this might make her overly nervous about ghosts too. Then I had an experience that gave me a sample of the feelings she might have in the church.

Three weeks after Julia's terrifying experiences, I was giving a talk in the church to the visiting members of a historical society from California's Mojave Desert. I told them some things about local history, and finished the talk by telling them some of the ghost stories. The president of their historical society then told some ghost stories he and other members of his family had experienced. The members of the desert historical society were very amiable and we chatted a good bit. After we finished, I began to take a booklet back to the office in the adjacent museum building.

Since the session had gone extremely well, I felt happy and calm as I was leaving the building, but suddenly I had a sensation of overwhelming terror for absolutely no reason. These feelings of overpowering fear and anxiety lasted for a few minutes---from the time I went to return the book to the office until I returned again to the church basement. Then, they suddenly disappeared and I felt fine again. The deeply disturbing emotions began as I walked by the storeroom that causes Tom and Denise such a feeling of dread, and ended after I passed again by the storeroom on my way back to the large room in the church basement.

I have had, on some other occasions in my life, vague feelings of fear or anxiety when there seemed to be no reasons for them, and I suppose that most people have done the same. But, I can't remember ever having had such intense feelings of terror happen so suddenly for no reason and then disappear so suddenly. Normally, I would assume that this happened because of some temporary brain anomaly, but, the fact that it occurred when I walked near the storeroom made me think that I may have experienced, just this once, the horrible feeling that Tom and Denise say they get from the storeroom. If the ghastly feeling I experienced near the storeroom is anything like what Denise says she feels there, it is no wonder she will never go near that room. She had also told of being suddenly overcome by such powerful feelings of depression when she walked into the pantry that she was not be able to shake off these feelings for a considerable time after she had returned to her home. I would imagine that if I picked up such appalling emotions from the ghosts in the church as Denise says she does, I would never go near the place again. I have often wondered why Tom and Denise sense the feeling of horror in the storeroom every time they are near it, while I have only sensed it once. I can't recall anything different about that day in comparison to the countless other days when I felt nothing there.

In addition to my inability to feel the emotions of ghosts, I often didn't react with strong fear because I generally assumed at first that supernatural sounds or scents were due to natural causes. It took time to investigate before I realized that there was nobody close by to make the sound of a voice, or sobbing, or whatever else I had heard, or to learn that there was nothing nearby to cause an odor. If a group of people was present, it also took time to find out that some of them who should have heard a very audible sound or smelled a very foul odor had not. By the time I became aware that it was not a normal sound or smell, the incident had already passed. It gave me a funny feeling when I realized it, but it was probably not as scary as if I had instantly recognized the true nature of my observation. I'm sure that my level of fear was also low because we spent so much time dealing with an appealing little girl ghost. A truly malevolent ghost or a headless ghost would undoubtedly be much scarier.

I was not unusual in my lack of fear when investigating ghosts. Tom brought groups of eager ghost-seekers to the church, and most of them walked around with a look of excitement on their faces and little or no evidence of any fear. He said that people in haunted houses often are so pleased to have a ghost that they don't want it to leave. People love fictional ghost stories because they are scary, but writing truthfully about real-life ghosts leaves one at a disadvantage because the real situations are not nearly so frightening as depicted in a Stephen King book. Although ghosts may seem terrifying to people who have never had experiences with them, those who actually encounter ghosts generally get the impression of very weak beings that have great difficulty in moving even small objects or in making themselves seen or heard by most people. Physically they appear to be just empty space. These limitations are due to their great difficulty in manifesting themselves in the physical world. Genuine terror comes from the most terrible physical threats such as erupting volcanoes, major earthquakes, tornadoes, terrorists, gang members, or a meeting with a grizzly bear in the wild, and ghosts seem extremely tame by comparison.

I imagine that if I read a book like mine when I was a skeptic about ghosts, I would assume that the author made up the stories to sell copies of the book. Skeptics probably will think the same of my book. If I were going to concoct a story to sell lots of books, I would have made the plot much scarier---maybe have one of the people in the historical society get killed by a ghost. In addition, there are many foolish-sounding things in the manuscript that I would have left out, like the hobo-type ghosts in the pantry. And I would have had the identities of all the ghosts made much clearer, rather than remaining so uncertain in most cases. It is no fun to read a novel when characters keep reappearing and you can't remember who they are, and it can be even more confusing to read a book about ghosts when there are a lot of ghosts and you don't even know the identities of most of them. The simple fact is that the events in this narrative happened exactly as I have recorded them.

A week after the meeting with the historical society from the desert, I had an eerie experience by the stage in front of the pews. I heard a creaking noise by the door that leads into the hallway behind the stage. It sounded like someone hurrying into the hallway. Then, after a short interval, I heard the sound of a door being slammed shut down the hallway. This gave me a creepy feeling since there was no one in the hallway or anywhere else nearby. As I mentioned in a previous chapter, the door of the groom's room, which is one of the doors down that hallway, opens by itself and sets off the burglar alarm when it has not been locked.

Then, on January 6, 1999, I saw something in the big, dark, naugahyde chair of the groom's room but it was not what I expected a ghost to look like. I was walking through the church with the dowsing rods, and seeing no movement anywhere. When I reached the hallway outside the groom's room, I aimed the dowsing rods at the closed door to the room. I was astounded to see the rods move. They had never shown movement for me in the groom's room before.

I opened the door, walked into the room, and was stunned by what I saw in the chair. The center of the chair looked intensely blurred, like you would see if you took a pair of binoculars and adjusted them so they were as far out of focus as possible. Outside of this central area, the rest of the chair and the room around it looked perfectly clear to me. The area of blurring did not have the outline of a body although it was the size of a person. I wondered if the center if my field of vision had become blurry as sometimes happens when I am developing a migraine headache. I looked away from the chair, aiming my gaze at other parts of the room, to see if my vision looked blurry in those directions too. Everything that I saw was perfectly clear when I looked in any other direction in the room, but each time that I looked at the chair it still had the intensely blurred area in it. It was as if there was an otherwise invisible object in the chair that affected the transmission of light through it so that it obscured what was behind it. I looked at the chair with disbelief. I thought, "This can't be happening!"

Tom has said that ghosts often appear to people as an ill-defined fuzzy form, and these images are frequently described as misty or fog-like. I would describe the image I saw as blurry-looking, because I think of mist or fog as appearing whitish under well-lighted conditions, and this blurry form had the same color as the dark chair behind it. Tom said life-like visions of ghosts wearing clothing are most likely produced by telepathy from the dead to the living.

I pointed the dowsing rods at the chair, and they jerked inward with shocking force, greater than I had ever felt before while using the rods. When I pointed them in other directions they moved but not nearly as strongly as when I aimed them at the chair. Lela Martin, who came with Tom's group when they explored the church, had told me that she sensed ghosts by reaching out to feel them. Lela had walked into the groom's room accompanied by her sister-in-law and her mother-in law. She said she sensed something in this chair, put her hand into it, and was able to see a boy in her mind's eye. Her sister-in-law agreed that it was a boy, but her mother-in-law thought the ghost was a man. Several other people who came to the church in April 1998 with Tom's group also said they sensed a ghost that was sitting in this chair.

I felt a combination of fright and intense curiosity, but the curiosity was the strongest. If Lela could put her hand into a ghost and survive, I could too. I didn't know if she just imagined the boy or not, but I shuddered, and then reached close to the chair to see what I would feel. The air by the chair felt icy, but no clear image of a boy, man, or anyone else popped into my head. After a couple of minutes had passed, the center of the chair no longer appeared blurry, and the rods no longer moved so vigorously when pointed at it. The rods still moved when pointed at the chair, and in various other directions, but now they moved at about the same rate when pointed at the chair or elsewhere in the room.

I left the room, making sure that the door was properly latched when I closed it. I did not tell Elizabeth what I experienced in the room, but said that I had carefully latched the door, but not locked it. She said since I was sure it was latched, she would not bother locking it this time. She set the alarm. I had hoped for this test to see if the door would come open when I was certain it was latched. Sure enough, after a passage of time, Elizabeth received a call from the burglar alarm company telling her the alarm had gone off. The groom's room door had come open.

After I had returned home from seeing the blurring in the chair, I was in a state of intense excitement for hours. I called several people on the telephone to tell them what I had seen. I had always wanted to see a ghost, expecting that it would look human-like, and had never expected to see anything like this.

My experiences in seeing the blurry form in the center of the chair reminded me that when Tom's group came to explore the old church, about nine months before my own experience, Mary Barnes said she saw a misty figure in the groom's room. I assumed that she saw a misty shape of a person, and when I next saw her at one of the meetings of Tom's group I asked her to give me more details of what she saw. I did not tell her what I had seen until I heard her reply. She said she saw a blurry form in the middle of the chair, and it did not have a clearly defined outline. Every where else she looked in the room was clear except for the blurred area in the chair. She thought, just as I did when I had the same experience, "Can I really be seeing this?" She couldn't believe her own eyes. I was amazed to hear that her experience was exactly like mine, and she was very startled when I told her I saw precisely the same thing she did. Irene, who was present when Mary saw the blurry form, had also seen it. Tom and Denise, at different times, had also seen the blurry-looking ghost in the groom's room. Two women who came to a tea at the church were to see it at a later time. Jan Hagman said she felt a male presence in the groom's room, and she saw him only as a dark silhouette. She told me she could see less details of his appearance than of any other ghost in the church.

Julia and Denise had each concluded there was an evil ghost in the groom's room. They had felt physically stricken when entering that room and could not have been convinced that this was merely due to the ghost of a mischievous boy.

Although the groom's room continued to be where visitors to the church most often reported sensing a ghost, it was not until September 9, 2000, one year and nine months after I had seen the image in the groom's room, that I had another experience by the groom's room. I decided to try my dowsing rods again in the church, even though I had not had them move there for many months.

I entered the church from the stairway on the south side about 11:30 AM. As I stepped into the entrance area by the panel where I was to deactivate the burglar alarm, I heard a man's loud voice very close to me. He was speaking excitedly as though he was making an exclamation, but I couldn't understand any words during the few seconds that I heard his voice. There was no man anywhere around who could have produced this voice. I had not seen any man outside when I walked into the church, there had been no car driving by on the side street at that time, and there was nobody across the street. There was certainly no man close to me, where the voice seemed to have originated. Was this the ghost from the groom's room? The voice came from the hallway that contains that room

I pointed the dowsing rods down the hallway in front of me, and the rods crossed each other vigorously. I did this repeatedly and they continued to move for about a minute. As I walked into the hallway I felt an intense chill. The air conditioner was not running. It was a warm summer day with temperatures that reached over 90 degrees and I later checked and found that every other part of the church felt much warmer than the hallway had when I first walked into it.

Twice before in the church I had heard voices, both female, coming from locations where no one was to be found. Once Elizabeth had been with me and also heard a voice. In each of these previous two cases, as on September 9, the voice sounded very close, but I could not make out any words. I asked Tom if it was possible that the voice was not actually speaking words. He said it is so difficult for people to communicate with spirits that it is quite common for people who hear a ghost to not be able to decipher the words.

Another strange event near where I heard the man's voice occurred about nine months later. Jean, a woman who had been president of the historical society before Elizabeth took over that role, and I were planning to enter the old church through the door at the top of the wooden stairs on the south side. When Jean tried to open the door she couldn't get it open. I tried, and felt and heard the lock open, but I couldn't pull the door open, no matter how hard I tried. After a couple of minutes I figured that it must be bolted from the inside.

We entered the building from another door and when we reached the inside of the door on the south side of the church I saw there was no bolt. Jean went outside, locked the door again, and then unlocked it and opened it easily. There didn't seem to be any possible natural explanation of why neither of us had been able to open it just before. Was this the ghost from the groom's room holding the door shut?

The incident had one interesting side benefit. I always wanted to ask Elizabeth's predecessor if she had any experiences with ghosts when she was president of the historical society, but I had never done so for fear that she might think the question was crazy. However, I noticed that when Jean and I were unable to open the door from outside, she got a frightened look on her face and she said, "It must have been the spirits."

When we were leaving the church later I did ask this ex-president of the Rialto Historical Society if she thought the church was haunted. After I had assured her that I believed it was, she told me that she thought so too. She said she felt a cold spot on the stairs leading down to the basement, said she felt a friendly female presence come near her when she played the organ during weddings, and said she had a lot of weird experiences during the five years that she had been president. She once was at the church talking with several people and the others were trying to recall someone's name. She said that she suddenly blurted out a name and it was the name that the people were trying to remember. She had never heard the name before in her entire life.

If a ghost held the door shut while I was trying to pull it open it was an extremely powerful ghost. How could a ghost exert such force? I recalled visiting a reported haunted house in Redlands, California where the owner told me he had once watched with disbelief as a heavily-loaded cardboard box weighing 80 or 90 pounds was pushed across a level floor by an unseen force. We know that the door to the groom's room comes open when left unlocked, so the groom's room ghost is the likely suspect for moving other things. Maybe he is the one who lifted up a very heavy old bathtub in the open space that is enclosed by high iron bars between the church and museum at the historical society and moved it 15 or 20 feet from where it had been sitting on some planks. Elizabeth, Jo, and Jean were befuddled one day when they came to the museum and found that the tub had been moved. One can't prove that a ghost moved it, but there had been no one around who would have hauled it to such a place. If the groom's room ghost can do these things, he might be dangerous.

15 It's Okay to Play a Prank on Tom

After so many encounters with ghosts in the church, I was increasingly puzzled by the lingering doubts I had, and I wondered why my feelings of uncertainty persisted so obstinately. After each ghostly experience, doubt began to creep back in the same way. When I observed a ghost, I was so excited that I had trouble getting to sleep that night. I would feel absolutely certain that ghosts are real. Then it would generally be quite a while until I had another such experience, since I tended to have only a few each year. I would go to the church repeatedly during the periods of time between ghost encounters without noticing anything out of the ordinary. My feelings of doubt about ghosts would start to return and my skeptical subconscious mind once again seemed to be getting the upper hand over the willing-to-believe conscious part of my mind. I went through this cycle of strong belief followed by increasing doubt time after time.

Skeptics claim that ghosts exist only in a person's imagination, but I had seen plentiful examples of two, three, four, or more people witnessing the same ghostly manifestations at the same time. I know these reports were not due to the power of suggestion, because nearly every time that I had experiences while a group of people was present, someone would mention the same thing that I had perceived before I had a chance to give my own account. I was always a bit hesitant to blurt out that I had observed a ghost. Neither could the reports be attributed to fear-induced overactive imaginations because one could clearly see that the majority of observers were fascinated by the ghosts rather than frightened of them.

The spooky incidents could not have been simply the work of a prankster. There were too many independent witnesses for this to be a hoax. More than 40 people have told me stories about their encounters with the ghosts of the old church. One woman who assists with weddings told me about being touched on the shoulder by a ghost during a wedding. A boy who came with his third grade class to tour the old church, came running down the hallway with terror on his face, shouting, "This place is haunted. I just saw the ghost of a woman." I certainly can't guarantee that all the claimed observations are correct.

94

A young couple once came to the church and said that they had attended a wedding at the church where many photographs were taken that showed ghosts posing with the wedding party. They said that nobody had seen these figures when the photos were taken. They told me that they had seen the photos themselves and everybody who was connected with the wedding was shocked by the photos. The young couple seemed very sincere in their awestruck descriptions of the photos. They offered to get copies of the photos to show me, and even though I was very doubtful that ghosts could show up in photos, I tried to make arrangements to see the photos but never managed to get in touch with the young couple again.

The earlier manifestations took place before I had contacted Tom, and he wasn't present when many of the later ones took place. There is no one or no group of people connected with the historical society who would or could pull off such sophisticated tricks.

In addition, there were plenty of examples where two or more people observed extraordinary manifestations at the same time, while others present, people whom I know to have acute senses, strong powers of observation, and excellent memories, were making every effort to note anything that happened, and experienced nothing. No prankster could produce such effects. For example, at the beginning of our first spirit communication session I heard an extremely loud noise and then heard Tom make a remark about it. Denise also heard the noise, but, astonishingly, ten of the thirteen people present heard nothing. Tom later said that it sounded like a two-by-four breaking in half, and it certainly did. If it had been a normal sound, such as would have been made by a prankster, everyone would have heard it.

Tom compared the inability of some people to detect ghosts to colorblindness. Based on my scrutiny of the multitude of people who have come to church over the last 15 years, including both one-time and infrequent visitors as well as those who spend a great deal of time there, clearly most can't sense the presence of ghosts. And most of those who have sensed the presence of ghosts in the church have detected them through other means than seeing them. People with the abilities to accurately see ghosts that Tom and Jan Hagman have are obviously extremely rare. A skeptic might say that those who can't discern ghosts are normal, while those who claim they can are a bunch of loonies. Those of us who observed the ghosts are far from loonies, however. All are rational and normal people, and some have truly outstanding minds. Tom and Jan Hagman would be very impressive people even if they had no psychic abilities at all. They are highly intelligent, are extremely perceptive observers of all sorts of things, are very successful in their careers, and are very knowledgeable collectors of unusual items.

Some of the people who have never sensed ghosts at the church have had ghostly experiences in other locations. One of the people who spent the most time at the church without ever having had an encounter with a ghost is Jean, a prominent member of the historical society. Jean, who is one of the most acute observers of life that I have ever known, wonders why she never had an experience at the historical society. Jean once did find she couldn't open the door on the south side of the church after unlocking it, as mentioned in the last chapter, but she can't believe this was due to a ghost. She would very much like to see, hear, feel, smell, touch, or otherwise sense a ghost in the church, but it has never happened.

Yet, Jean has stories to tell about encounters with the spirits of her own departed loved ones. She heard the characteristic limping sounds of her deceased father's footsteps in their old family home, and she once saw her husband, looking happy and full of life again, after his death. On two different occasions I took Jean home and smelled a strong whiff of cigarette smoke when we entered the house. Jean's husband was a smoker who died of lung cancer. Nobody had smoked in the house in years, and there was never a scent of cigarette smoke at other times. On another occasion Jean was walking down a hallway in her house after returning from a trip and she smelled the strong and pleasant smell of her husband's unique blend of pipe tobacco. Tom said that a ghost goes to the most psychic person available to show itself or to try to get help, but he added that Jean observed the presence of her deceased relatives because they have a special bond to her.

Readers of ghost stories and attendees of ghost movies may get the idea that people in a haunted building have supernatural experiences in an almost nonstop fashion. If my experiences in the old church are typical for someone with limited ability to sense ghosts, such a person would have to spend an enormous amount of time in a haunted building to expect to have some memorable experiences. I don't know what was different about those rare days when I would sense a ghost, but maybe the ghosts made an extra effort at those times to get through to me. It would take the powers of a Tom or Jan Hagman to walk into a haunted building and to start having experiences with ghosts right away. A person who makes a single visit of a few hours to a reported haunted house is very unlikely to come across a ghost. I have been in the groom's room more times than I could count, but I have never noticed anything strange in that room except on the one occasion when I saw the blurry apparition in the chair.

Most people, as we have seen, don't have the ability to sense a ghost no matter how much time they spend in a haunted building. The best they can hope for is to be able to observe things moved, opened or closed, turned on or off, etc., in cases where no natural explanation appears possible. A few people who have spent a lot of time in the old church, but who have never been able to sense the ghosts, regard the claims of ghosts as a lot of nonsense.

I visited a haunted house in Redlands with Tom and Jan, and the couple who lived there said that incidents happened about once a month. I never had any ghostly experiences when I visited the house with Tom and Jan. Tom has said that many people who live in a haunted house would notice nothing. If they did notice something, they often would assume that their mind must be playing tricks on them, or that there must be some natural explanation even though they can't imagine what it would be.

In addition to the powerful evidence of ghosts that I was experiencing in the church I was also hearing impressive amounts of evidence about ghosts in other places than the church. When I first became interested in the ghosts in the church, I told very few people about them, but later I began to discuss the ghosts with quite a lot of people. These were people who had not been connected with the church, and I was very surprised to find out how many of them had their own ghost stories. Some people would immediately reply to my stories by telling their own ghost stories, but many others would ask, "Do you really believe in ghosts?" Not until I answered yes would they tell me their own stories. I learned that even people whom I had known for many years had ghost stories that they had never told me until they saw that I would take them seriously. Whether they all had actually encountered a ghost is another question. Tom has said that during the many times he has been called to investigate haunted houses, most often he finds that the house does not actually contain a ghost.

More than sixty people who have never had any connection with the old church told me ghost stories about their own experiences. I don't know exactly what percentage this represents of all the people that I talked to about ghosts, but it would be a considerable minority of them. I don't trust polling data to determine accurately what percentage of people think they have encountered a ghost. I imagine that many people wouldn't want to admit this even to a stranger on the telephone, unless the stranger had made it clear to them that he or she believed in ghosts. The fear of ridicule about believing in ghosts is very powerful in most people. Many of the people whose experiences with ghosts are discussed in this manuscript have told me that they did not want their full names to be revealed.

When I was a total skeptic about ghosts, before having my experiences in the church or hearing my cousin's story about the ghost in his family's mountain cabin, I assumed that only foolish or insane people would ever think they had met up with a ghost. All of the people who told me of their experiences with ghosts in other places than the old church seemed very rational, and some are extremely impressive individuals. One was a distinguished scientist and professor at the University of California at Riverside. Another had been Rialto City Attorney for many years before becoming a highly respected judge in San Bernardino County, California. He is an expert on evaluating evidence, and he is convinced that he encountered a ghost. Another is a beloved local woman who, like the historical society's president, Elizabeth, has a school named after her for her outstanding voluntary community service. One of my old college friends is now chairman of the math department at a prestigious eastern university, and he has given me accounts of his brother's ghost. I learned it is a very bad assumption to think that only foolish people have ghost stories to tell.

Tom told me that men do most of the investigating of the paranormal, but most of the people who tell of their supernatural experiences are women. He said that many more men than women are embarrassed to admit that they have had an encounter with a ghost. The great majority of people who told me their own ghost stories were women.

It appeared that my lifelong skepticism had become such an ingrained part of my thinking that it would not let go of its grip on me, and I wondered how much more time and how much more evidence would be needed before the doubts would vanish. Maybe I would never be able to eliminate them. Some people would consider a belief in ghosts to be irrational, but my difficulty to totally believe in ghosts seemed irrational to me, considering the enormous amount of convincing evidence I had observed or heard about. My doubts led to an overpowering compulsion to discover more evidence for ghosts. Each time Tom came to the church, I would look forward to the meeting with a tremendous sense of anticipation. I would be so eager to see what would happen, and so filled with excitement, that time seemed to slow down agonizingly as I counted the days until the next meeting. I could never get enough evidence for the existence of ghosts to satisfy me, and I was always looking for more. My feelings of doubt were to remain for a long time.

Even if I had felt certain that ghosts are real, I still had another doubt in my mind. What if ghosts are not conscious true spirits of the dead, but are instead some inexplicable preserved trace of the past which are observable under certain conditions by certain people---like seeing a videotape from the past being replayed? Tom said that a spirit may be gone, but spirit or memory traces called shells may still be present. He told me that a sensitive person may activate these shells, and it is not always apparent whether one is dealing with a spirit or just memory forms. He said if doors are opened or objects are moved it is a sign that a spirit is there and not a shell.

After all the strange things that had been happening in the church, I was very anxious to find out what Tom would conclude if he returned for another investigation. I asked him if he would be willing to do this, and he said that although he tended to lose sensitivity and accuracy over time as he continued to investigate a haunted building he would be willing to give it a try. He asked to be allowed to go through the church by himself as he made the investigation, because he might get confused results if he went through the building with someone else and picked up things from them rather than from a ghost.

Tom had told of the mischievous ghost of a boy who liked to play tricks on people in the church. I decided to ask out loud in the church for a ghost or ghosts to play a trick on Tom. I went into the hallway by the groom's room and announced in a loud voice that Tom would be coming in a few days, and if any ghost had a message to give to him this would be the time to do it. Then I added, "It's okay to play a trick on Tom." I didn't really expect this to happen, but I extended the invitation to any ghosts who could hear me on the unlikely chance that I would actually see a trick played on Tom. If I did, that could indeed indicate that ghosts have consciousness.

Tom arrived at 4:45 PM on a gloomy, chilly, drizzly April day in 1999. We went to the groom's room, sat down, and began to talk. Tom said that the ghosts liked to come into the groom's room because they can see their own reflections in the mirror. The sight of their images shows them they truly exist. He thought that if we had just the right light at the right moment, we might be able to see their reflections too. His comments about the mirrors were interesting to me, because Denise had previously remarked, at a time when Tom was not present, that the mirrors in the groom's room were very disturbing to her. She told me she had once seen enough in the reflection of the mirror in the groom's room that she didn't want to see any more. She didn't seem to want to elaborate on what she had seen, so I didn't ask for any more details. Elizabeth told me Denise saw the reflection of a blurry form in the chair.

While Tom and I were talking in the groom's room, he was sitting in the big naugahyde chair where Mary Barnes and I each saw the blurry apparition, and I was sitting in another chair opposite him.

100

Then we got up to go take a look at the bride's room just to the south of the groom's room. Ever since I saw the apparition in the naugahyde chair I have always glanced at that chair whenever I am in the groom's room in case I would suddenly see the same sight again. I took a look at the chair as I followed Tom out of the room and saw nothing in it.

After Tom finished looking in the bride's room, we walked down the hallway again and went back into the groom's room. We were both astonished to see a dime perched on the center front part of the seat of the chair. He exclaimed, "What's that?" I was certain it had not been there when we left the groom's room a short time before. Tom sat in the naugahyde chair and tried to figure out if the coin could have fallen out of his pocket, since he had some coins in his left pants pocket. He said that if it fell out of his pocket while he was sitting in the chair, it would have landed farther back on the left side of the chair and not at the front of its center. Then Tom saw something on the floor in the corner of the room to the right of the chair. His eyes were nearly popping out of his head as he picked up a small paper-wrapped object and said it was the medicine he was carrying in his left pants pocket. Tom had never been to the right of the chair. Because the medicine was in his left trousers pocket, he said that it couldn't possibly have fallen out of his pocket and landed to the right of the chair. Tom said he was sure he hadn't put his hands in his pants pockets since he arrived at the church. He put his keys in his jacket pocket rather than his pants pocket.

As we talked, I made a sketch of the chair and the footstool in front of it, showing the location of the dime on the chair and the medicine on the floor. I looked up at Tom as I spoke to him, and then looked down again as I finished my sketch. I was amazed to see a coin directly in front of the footstool that had not been there an instant before. This was a penny that seemingly appeared by magic.

Could Tom have scattered the coins and medicine around to fool me? I don't think that would be possible because I am certain the dime on the chair wasn't there when we left the room. As I was following Tom out of the room I took my customary glance at the chair to see if there was a blurry form in it. I certainly would have noticed if there was a shiny dime on the chair at that time. When we returned to the groom's room, we both saw the dime when we were still quite some distance from the chair. It is possible that during my first visit to the groom's room I might not have noticed the medicine if it had already been on the floor, but the penny appeared in front of the footstool after not having been there an instant before. I had looked down in that exact spot as I made my sketch of the chair and footstool, seen nothing there, looked up at Tom, then looked back down, and saw the penny. At the time that the penny suddenly appeared on the floor in front of the footstool, Tom was on the opposite side of the footstool from me, and not in any position to drop or toss the penny into its location immediately in front of the footstool.

Tom said he was a little spooked, as the incidents took him completely by surprise, and he had never experienced anything like this before. He told a story about a little girl who had died, and when her spirit came around her family found dimes. Tom said that ghosts sometimes make objects suddenly materialize by a process called teleportation. Tom guessed that the ghost boy had played the tricks with the coins and the medicine. He was not worried because he felt the boy was mischievous, and was just having some fun.

I told Tom that a couple of days before he arrived to investigate the church I had announced in the church that he would be coming on Monday. I said if the ghosts wanted help or had any message to give him he would be able to see and hear them, and that they should get their message to Tom then or forever hold their peace. Tom was surprised to hear I did this.

I did not tell Tom then that before his visit I also announced in the church that it would be okay if the ghosts played a prank on him. I wasn't sure how Tom would react if I told him about this. I did not tell Tom about my invitation for the ghosts to play a prank on him until six months after this visit. He was startled by my admission, and said, "Did you really do that?" He didn't seem angry that I had done this, however.

After Tom left the church on that Monday evening, I secured all of the doors, including carefully locking the groom's room, set the burglar alarm, and left. The next Saturday there was a wedding in the church. Elizabeth said that after the wedding the footstool was beside

102

the chair and they were not in their normal location in the corner of the room. She always checks the position of the chair after weddings, because if it is moved away from the corner and toward the west along the north wall of the room, it tends to leave scrape marks on the wall when it is used. Therefore she always moves the chair and footstool back into the northeast corner of the room if they are out of place. She clearly remembered doing this on the Saturday night after the wedding.

Four days after the wedding, on the following Wednesday, Elizabeth and I opened the door to the groom's room. Elizabeth was very startled to see that the chair and footstool had been shifted well to the west of the northeast corner of the room. Elizabeth felt certain nobody had been in the room from the night of the wedding until we unlocked the door. Since the door is opened for weddings and wedding rehearsals, for cleaning, or for groups touring the building, and because none of these things had happened since the wedding on Saturday night, Elizabeth could feel very confident that the door had not been opened. Also, I checked with the very few people who have access to the special key that opens the groom's room, and all of them assured me they had not been in the room between the time of the wedding and the time that Elizabeth and I opened the door.

The inexplicable movement of the chair in the groom's room was not the only strange case of something being moved in the old church. Earlier, the spare key to the groom's room, which is hidden in a drawer in a piano bench, disappeared. Elizabeth and another lady who use it during weddings were mystified by its disappearance. After it had been missing for a couple of weeks, it suddenly reappeared in the drawer. I hadn't even known of its existence until Elizabeth told of its disappearance, and there are no plausible suspects who would have taken it for two weeks and then returned it.

The weird things that happened to Tom after I had requested the ghosts to play a trick on him amazed me so much that I was anxious to see what would happen if I asked the ghosts to play a trick when another visitor came to the church. I got my chance before too long. One day in February 2000, I received a call from a man named Wes whom I had not heard from for almost twenty years. He had been my supervisor when I was a soil scientist with the U.S. Bureau of Land Management, and he was calling to find out the telephone number of another man who had also worked in the same BLM office. After I had given him the number, he asked what I had been doing. When I told him that I had been investigating ghosts in an old church and writing a book about the subject, he immediately showed great interest and asked if he could visit the church some time. I told him to call me when he wanted to visit, and I would arrange to give him a tour. He said he had never had an experience in his life that convinced him he had encountered a ghost (he was 70 years old), and was curious to see what he would experience in the church.

A few weeks later he called, and we arranged to meet at the church on the afternoon of March 15, 2000. I did not tell Wes any details about the ghosts before his arrival, so it would be possible to see what he could sense on his own. A few days before Wes arrived, I stood in the church and appealed to the unseen spirits to do something so powerful when he was there that he would be convinced that they truly existed.

He arrived at about three in the afternoon on a very warm March day, with a high temperature of 84 degrees listed in the local paper. I led him to a door at the top of the wooden stairs on the south side of the church. I unlocked the door, but, as happened in the previous chapter when Jean and I tried to enter through this door, it would not open. I was certain that I had the right key and had turned it correctly, and I could hear and feel the door unlock when I turned the key. The door just wouldn't budge. Wes said, "Maybe the ghosts don't want me in there." I struggled for a couple of minutes with the door and suddenly it opened very easily. Later, after Wes had left, I repeatedly locked and unlocked this same door without having any trouble opening it.

After Wes came into the church, I first took him into the groom's room to see if he could sense anything. He said he didn't see or hear any ghosts, and joked that he must have scared them off. We next walked through the sanctuary and then down the stairs leading to the basement of the church, and still he said he didn't notice anything strange. When we reached the doorway between the stairway and the basement he suddenly had a very startled look on his face.

Wes said he felt a chill, although the day was very warm. He said that he had a very strange feeling down his back. He reported seeing two pulses of light by a painting on the darkened wall on the opposite side of the big room. He said the first pulse was about six inches or so in diameter and not extremely bright. Then he saw a fainter flash of light to the right of where he had seen the first pulse. He kept opening and closing the door between the stairs and the basement to see if this allowed light to shine onto the wall, but the wall stayed dark.

I hadn't seen the flashes of light on the wall that Wes reported. Maybe I wasn't looking at the right spot. I wondered if the creepy sensation down his back was just due to his own feeling that a ghost was in the room. We walked through the basement room, went across the small entrance way to the east of this room, continued through the adjacent kitchen and pantry rooms, and then walked into the hallway, restroom, and storeroom areas to the north of the kitchen. Wes didn't notice anything unusual in any of the places to the east of the large basement room.

We returned to the large basement room again, and Wes starting squirming and writhing. He said he had the weird feeling in his back again. He was obviously very alarmed, and said that his legs felt like they were getting weak, and he had to get out of the room while his legs still worked. He rushed up the stairs, and then told me that he wouldn't ever want to go back down there again. This resolve never to return to the basement room did not last too long, since Wes returned to the room during future visits.

A few hours after Wes had left the church, he sent me an email describing his experiences. He wrote, "On the way home I tried to rationalize what I experienced in the basement. The light on the wall could be my imagination wanting to see or feel something [it might also be light reflected from passing cars]. But the sensation that I felt in my back and legs and the need to get out of the room were completely foreign. I am convinced that something supernatural is going on in that basement."

I asked him what the sensation felt like in his back, and he wrote, "The feeling in my back is almost impossible to explain. More like an intensive tingling limited to my spine from neck to the base of the backbone. It was not like a shiver that one experiences with cold air. I also had a sensation that I must get out of the room and I don't know how that can be interpreted. I was about six feet from the door and I think I felt disconnected from my legs, like it was hard to get them to get me to the door. Once outside all sensations disappeared."

After Wes's adventures in the church basement, I told him about the investigations of the church ghosts, and the role of the spirit investigator, Tom Hagman. To my surprise, Wes recognized Tom's name. Both served as officers of a Credit Union in an adjacent city. I had never suspected that they knew each other, and Wes was amazed to learn of Tom's ghost investigating, since Tom had never mentioned it to him. Soon afterward, Tom was surprised to see Wes come into his office for a visit. After a bit of small talk, he told Tom that he believed he had had a supernatural experience and he wanted to talk to Tom about things that had gone on in the church.

Tom could not believe that it was just coincidence that Wes had called me after having been out of touch for 20 years, or that Wes had turned up in his office. Had it been arranged to show Wes that there is another side?

Shortly after Wes's visit, Tom brought a group to the church that included a married couple named Stan and Cheryl who had been to the church before. Stan had once been a Baptist Minister, but had since become a counselor for drug addicts. His wife Cheryl is a cute brunette. Tom told me to ask the ghosts to do something to the group, but said that I should not even tell him what I had requested. The next time I was in the church I asked the ghosts to give a very convincing demonstration of their existence when Tom's group showed up.

When Tom's group came to the church they first gathered in the big basement room, and then headed off to investigate various parts of the church. Cheryl spent quite a while upstairs, but decided to return to the basement room where she had left her purse on a chair. When she reached the table she was surprised to see her purse had been moved. She wondered who had moved it, but later everyone denied moving it.

It had been on the chair at the northwest corner of a large table and it was now on a chair at the southeast corner of the same table. Cheryl returned her purse to the chair at the northwest corner of the table, and then walked away from the table. When she returned to the table a minutes later she was astounded to see her purse once again on the chair at the southeast corner of the table. She said she had been in sight of the room during the time when the purse was moved a second time, saw nobody come into the room, and knew that none of the people in the building could have moved it this second time. Tom said that Cheryl had often asked him, "Why doesn't anything ever happen to me?" Apparently the spirits had heard my request to give a demonstration of their existence, and they gave the demonstration to the person who needed it most. Cheryl looked very scared.

Another visit came when a neighbor of mine, Polly, toured the church with her mother, Mary. Again, before their scheduled visit I made a request in the empty church for them to be given a demonstration that the ghosts were there. They were both astounded by the movement of the dowsing rods in their hands. Polly, who said she had seen a ghost in her house when she lived in El Monte, California, reported that she felt the presence of a spirit in the church that gave her a pleasant feeling. In one place Polly felt a tingling in her palms as the dowsing rods moved, and in another location, the movement of the rods was accompanied by a tingling in her fingers. She said that the rods produced vibrations. Suddenly we heard a loud, metallic noise that sounded like it came from very close by in the middle of the pews. It did not have a muffled quality, as it would have if it had come from outside. The noise was a combination of "bong" and "click" sounds at the same time. It was a very strange noise, and one that I had never heard during many hours spent in the sanctuary. Polly said, it was like a message saying, "We are here."

After the contents of Tom's pockets had been scattered in the groom's room, he said the ghost of a mischievous boy had done it. I wondered if the same ghost had also given the demonstrations of its existence to Wes, Cheryl, and Polly. I certainly had the feeling that one or more ghosts had listened to my requests and then carried them out in a very different manner in each case.

I can't guarantee that all of these people who toured the church in search of encounters with ghosts really had them, but they seemed convinced that they had. I told Tom about them, and related that in each case I had asked the ghosts to show the ghost seekers evidence that ghosts truly exist. Tom said, "You could charge people to come and have experiences after asking the spirits to give them demonstrations." After seeing what happened when I asked the ghosts to show themselves off to other people, I began to beseech them to give me performances too.

Sometimes new visitors to the old church got some powerful evidence of the ghosts without my asking for it. On Saturday, September 23, 2006, Ronnie Featherstone and his sister, Marilyn Featherstone Forney, came to the Rialto Historical Society to tell humorous stories about growing up in Rialto to a group of nearly 40 present and former Rialto residents. When Ronnie first came into the old church building he gave Jean Randall a big hug. Then he bent down to look at some historical displays near the floor. He felt a rush of air past his right year and thought that Jean Randall might be blowing air by his ear. He looked around and saw that she was standing some distance behind him. He bent down to look again and once more felt a rush of air past his ear. He didn't give this much thought because he figured there was a draft in the building or a cooler vent nearby. Ronnie didn't tell me anything at that time about this incident or other peculiar incidents that followed that day. Neither he nor his sister, Marilyn, mentioned the strange things that they experienced until a week or so later.

I began to show Ronnie the old telephone switchboard in the storeroom just to the north of the stairs that lead from the church basement up to the pews upstairs. I knew that he would be interested to see it because his mom had been a telephone switchboard operator for years. Ronnie was to tell me later that every time that he touched the keyboards or switches, they felt bitterly cold. This seemed odd to him because it was a warm day.

Then, Ronnie started up the stairs that lead to the church sanctuary. He was walking by himself and thus was suddenly very startled when he felt somebody pushing him from behind. He looked behind him but nobody was there. When he reached the main church congregation area, he saw that he was alone, and, as he looked around, memories came flooding back to him of the times that he attended the church during his youth. He walked up onto the stage, sat down at the piano, and began to play. He was shocked to feel somebody pushing his hands down onto the keys, because there was nobody there but himself.

Now, Ronnie had no doubt that something really strange was going on. Still not telling anybody what he had experienced, he began to set up some displays on the stage at the front of the pews. Ronnie had been a member of the Deacon's Car Club of Rialto during the 50s and early 60s, and he hung a Deacon's T-shirt, a Deacon's jacket, and some other Deacon's memorabilia from a rack that he had placed on the stage. The audience started to file in a short time later. Ronnie's brother-in-law, Jack Forney, began to take photos of the Deacon's display.

When Jack's photos were sent to me as email attachments a few days later, I shared them with others in our Internet Rialto alumni websites. The woman who set up the Internet groups, Diane Funderburg Deam, pointed out that there were orbs in the photos. There was a small orb just to the left of the Deacon's jacket on the stage and a much bigger one just to the right of the Deacon's T-shirt. There were also orbs in photos of the audience. There were additional orbs in the photos of the group taken downstairs in the church basement before they came up to hear the talk in the church sanctuary. Some ghost investigators regard the presence of orbs in photographs as showing the presence of ghosts, whereas skeptics scoff at the idea and dismiss orbs is just an anomaly of the photographic process.

Shortly after Ronnie began to talk, he introduced his sister, Marilyn, who joined him on the stage. They began to tell their stories to the alumni group. Days later, when I emailed the photo attachments to Marilyn that showed the orbs, she replied with details of her own incredible experience. Marilyn wrote, "I had a very weird experience when we were on stage. I was on the right side (the right side of the view from the audience). Several times while we were up there, I tried to move to the left side of the stage and couldn't. It was like there was a wall there and I bumped into it when trying to move. It was a very strange feeling."

Ronnie and the Deacons seem to attract orbs. On Saturday, Mar. 31, 2007, a Rialto Junior High School reunion was held for alumni of the 50s at the El Rancho Verde Country Club in North Rialto. The orbs showed up in even greater numbers than in the church photos when photographed by several different photographers at the country club. It was only the photos taken of Ronnie standing with the other members of the Deacons Car Club that were loaded with orbs.

16 Don't Turn on the Lights

I had finished what I assumed to be a completed manuscript about the ghosts in the old church, and I called Tom to say I was ready to give it to him to review. We arranged to meet for dinner at a Mexican restaurant just south of the church, so I could give the text to him and then enjoy an evening of his conversation. But I took the keys to the old church when I went to the restaurant in the hope that Tom would agree to once again examine it.

As Tom and I were having dinner, I pulled the church keys out of my pocket, showed them to him, and asked him if he would be willing to make another visit to the church. Tom said he was hoping I would ask. When we entered the church, I asked Tom if I should turn on all of the lights, as we had always done before when he had come to the church during the evening. Tom said, "Don't turn on the lights." He explained that it was often easier to sense ghosts in dim light. I had my flashlight, and we turned on only enough scattered lights to allow us to move about safely in the darkened church.

Tom walked into the bride's room, where he stayed for a very short time. Then he walked into the groom's room, sat down, and remained for a long time with his eyes closed. He said, "You don't hear anything? You don't hear the sobbing?" I didn't hear anything. Tom said he heard a girl sob, and then heard her say, "It's over now," as though she was never coming back to the church again. He said there was sadness in the words.

Tom left the groom's room and sat for a while in a pew toward the front of the sanctuary. Then he had a sudden urge to go downstairs to the church basement. As we walked down the steps to the church basement and reached Kristina's display case beside the bottom of the stairs, Tom noticed that two of the objects in the cabinet had fallen outward against the glass. One was a framed photograph of Kristina, and the other, immediately to the left of the photo, was a board on which Kristina had painted a small portrait of herself. When we went into the church basement, we saw that the light was on in the toy-filled room just to the south of the wall containing Kirstina's display case. This was Kristina's favorite room according to Tom. He was astounded. He thought that the tipped over portraits in the display case and the light in Kristina's favorite room must be connected with Kristina somehow.

Elizabeth and Jean later said that they believed a recent earthquake had tipped over the portraits. They also said that a couple of people had been working in the church basement recently and one of these people probably forgot to turn off the light in the room with all the toys. Tom replied that of all the many things that might have been tipped over in the church by an earthquake, why did this happen only to the two portraits of Kristina? He also said that of all the lights that could have been left on, why did it happen to be the light in her favorite room that was lit? He thought these things were more than coincidence.

Tom next sat in a white wicker chair. After sitting for quite a while in the chair with his eyes closed, he suddenly nearly jumped out of the chair, and said, "Somebody is here. They just blew on my face. Their breath went right across my face." I didn't feel anything except a slight draft of cool air. Tom said, "I'm asking to know who it is." After a short time, He said that someone had blown across his face two more times.

Then we heard a strange metallic noise coming from the big basement room. It sounded like two pieces of metal hitting together. We walked into the basement room, looked around, and headed for the door that leads into the entryway to the kitchen. Tom said he had bad feelings about what was on the other side of the door. He said, "I can't go in there."

But after a brief hesitation, he opened the door. I smelled a strong and very pleasant odor, which vanished so quickly that I did not have a chance to characterize it in my mind. Tom later compared it to the heaviness of the odors in a tobacco shop, although he said it was not a tobacco odor. It was a very peculiar odor because there was no apparent natural source for it, and because strong, natural odors don't just instantly vanish in still air.

Tom was sitting in a chair in the entryway, thinking about all this, when we both heard a loud metallic thud back of the kitchen. He described it as sounding like someone kicking a metal trash can. The two of us went in the direction of the noise, and he told me that he got a terrible feeling from being near the storeroom. It felt to him like an electrical current was going up his back and across his shoulders.

Then Tom went back to the entryway and sat down again. Suddenly, he said, "Look at that!" He was pointing at an artificial leaf that was lying on the floor in the doorway to the large basement room. I had not seen the leaf on the floor when we walked into the entryway from the large room, and this was one area of the church that was very well lit after I turned on the light on our way into the entryway. Tom said that he had stood in the big basement room and observed everything carefully before we went into the entryway, and he was certain that the leaf had not been there. The plastic leaf had come from an artificial plant that was sitting on an organ to the south of the doorway. It was too far away from the organ to have reached its location by falling off the plant, and there was no chance of it having been carried there by a draft.

In a horribly tragic accident a few months before, Tom lost his only child. She was hit by a car while trying to save the life of an injured cat that was lying in the street. Tom was later to tell me that he kept finding snipped off leaves on the floor of his house after her memorial service. At first he thought it was his dog that was pulling the leaves off the plants, but then he noticed that the leaves only came off the plants from her funeral. Now a ghost apparently had placed a leaf right in front of us in the doorway.

We went back upstairs to prepare to leave, and talked just inside the exit door about what had happened. Tom said the ghosts had lured us along a path through the church by use of the tilted portraits, the light in Kristina's favorite room, the noises in the church basement, and the leaf on the floor. He told me that this is the way ghosts often grab people's attention. He believed that the communications were intended for me. He guessed that the ghosts knew I had completed my book and had asked him to take one last look at the church, and that they were letting me know that there was still someone or something there. He thought they wanted to prove to me beyond a reasonable doubt that their world exists.

Just then, I heard the whimper of a child's voice directly behind me. I said, "Could that have come from outside?" Tom immediately opened the outside door, and we could see that there were no children anywhere in sight. A little further thought made it obvious that this little whimper could not have come from outside, because earlier we had found that it required a loud yell to penetrate the church walls. Also we agreed that it was definitely the sound of a child's voice, and not some inanimate sound that we imagined was a child. The whimper came just after Tom told me the spirits wanted to prove that the other side exists and that it came right on cue. The whimper I heard sounded like a little girl. Tom's impression was that this was the same ghost he heard sobbing earlier in the groom's room. He did not know the identity of the ghost, but did not feel that Kristina was back in the building

Still in awe of this experience, we both walked into the darkened sanctuary rather than leaving the church. Tom sat down in one of the pews, and I sat to his right and behind him to watch him. Then, to our left, while we were both sitting quietly in the pews, I heard the extremely loud, cracking and creaking noises that one hears when someone sits down on one of the ancient pews. It sounded exactly like the noise that Tom and I had just made when each of us sat down. Shortly, Tom said, "It is gone now." He said he didn't know who the ghost was. But we were both sure that the pews never make a noise like that unless someone sits on them.

On a later occasion, I once again heard the sounds of someone sitting down in the pews when Tom and I were seated in the church with no other living person present. Tom had suddenly issued a spoken challenge to the ghosts to use his energy to give us evidence that they truly existed; and we quickly heard an astonishing variety of sounds that clearly came from very close by in the sanctuary. These included the familiar drawn-out creaking sound of somebody sitting on a pew followed a few seconds later by the identical sound of another person sitting on a pew. We also heard clicking sounds, bumping sounds, and rustling sounds. We heard loud rapping sounds on the wall of the church near where we were sitting at the southeast corner of the sanctuary and the rapping noises proceeded to move westward toward the front of the church and then northward across the back wall of the church. Tom also said he heard the sounds of somebody moaning, but I did not hear it. We both heard the unmistakable sounds of footsteps passing by us. After we went into the basement of the church, we both smelled a strong scent of incense (there wasn't any being produced) and then the odor instantly disappeared.

I had a fascinating experience with disembodied footsteps on another occasion when Tom came to the church with the group that meets with him on the second Thursday evening of each month. Tom, Cheryl, and I arrived early, and as we were waiting for the others we heard the sound of footsteps on the concrete entryway just below the steps that lead down into the church basement from the southeast side of the church. The door was open, and I waited to see who would appear. The footsteps sounded to me like they belonged to a woman. When we looked, nobody was there or anywhere else around.

I had more work to do on my book.

17   Visits at Home from Some Church Ghosts?

During my investigations of ghosts in the old church, there were times when such strange things happened in my home that I wondered if the ghosts sometimes followed me there, as Tom predicted might happen. I mentioned earlier about times when Kristina seemed to have come to my home resulting in my mother hearing the footsteps of an unseen child. I had another experience that I thought might result from Kristina's presence when I heard an unseen girl's voice near my computer. In addition, I smelled a delicious perfumed scent for which I could find no natural source while writing in my notebook about how much Kristina liked to write.

Other bizarre events have happened at my home in addition to the incidents that I have previously mentioned. In May 1999, I started to hear strange noises around my bedroom at night. There were tapping sounds on the walls and occasionally other eerie noises, such as the sound of clicks coming from the computer as though someone was typing. Sometimes these sounds gave me a chilly feeling, because I never heard anything like them before. Once, the tapping noises first started on the wall opposite my bed and then progressively moved across the intervening wall until I heard them directly behind my pillow. This really gave me the willies.

The noises would generally begin between midnight and about 3 AM, and would continue for a period ranging from a few seconds up to as long as quite a few minutes. Sometimes, I would turn on the outside light and rush out with my flashlight, and even climb on the roof and look into the attic. One time long before I became aware of the ghostly incidents at the old church, I heard thumping noises in the attic. I climbed on the roof, shined my flashlight into the attic, and saw a possum that had entered through an unseen hole. I don't think the more recent sounds were due to a possum or any other animal because they were coming mostly from the sides of the walls, several feet above the ground, rather than from the roof or attic. They did not have the sharp sound of a bird pecking on wood, and they did not come strictly from locations where birds could perch. There were times when it would sound like something was rubbing against the wall. The tapping and rubbing noises came from different parts of the walls, occasionally from the attic, and sometimes they seemed to be right next to my head by the pillow. I continued to hear noises on quite a few nights on into July 1999. After that, the noises stopped. Despite, all of my efforts to find the cause, I never could figure it out.

An even stranger incident happened when I was getting up from bed on the morning of March 24, 1999, and grabbed my jeans, which were folded over the arm of a chair. As I pulled them up to put them on, I was astounded when I saw that not only were my shorts still in my pants, they were positioned in the top of my jeans and stretched out in all directions. They looked just like an invisible person was wearing them.

I always remove my shorts and place them in a separate place to add to the laundry when I take them off before going to bed, and I never leave them in my pants. This incident involved more than just forgetting to remove my shorts from my pants, however. The amazing thing was that they were filled out inside my pants exactly as if someone was wearing them.

I experimented by taking off my pants and leaving my shorts in them. The elastic band in the shorts caused them to wad up, and then they would fall down the pants leg when I lifted the pants as I would before putting them on. Could I have also grabbed my shorts when I grabbed my pants, and thus caused them to spread out inside the pants? I tried experimenting with this also, and found that the elastic caused them to stretch between my two hands, and not be spread out in all directions, as they were when I originally picked up the pants. I made drawings showing the appearance of my shorts inside my jeans when I first saw them, and have very detailed notes about the incident.

In May 1999, my mother had an experience that is also very hard to explain. She went into her bathroom very early in the morning. She heard a rumbling sound similar to the sound that occurs when I am pulling a trash barrel up our walkway, but I wasn't up yet. She looked down and saw a big bunch of toilet paper on the floor, and the toilet paper roll was unrolling by itself. There was an inch or so of paper still left on the roll. She said the funny thing about all of this was she had not touched the roll of toilet paper. A few days later she saw the same thing happen again. She said it eventually happened six or eight times.

This reminded me of the time I went with Tom and Jan Hagman to investigate a reported haunted house in Redlands, California in November 1997. The husband of the young woman who was being tormented by the ghosts said he twice saw a roll of toilet paper unroll before his eyes until there was nothing left on the holder except a bare cardboard tube. He said each time this happened, there was initially about one-fourth of a roll. The only time toilet paper can unroll by itself is when the paper is almost completely gone so the paper hanging down from the tube is relatively heavy compared to the weight of the cardboard tube and small amount of toilet paper still on the tube. This was not the case when either my mother or the man in Redlands had seen toilet paper unrolling by itself.

.   I also had a very strange experience at home with the dowsing rods a couple of years earlier. I tried the dowsing rods many times in my house without getting any movement. But, in December 1997, the rods did move when I used them in the house. They first moved at 1:15 PM when I pointed them at a rocking chair in the living room. I aimed them in other directions and also found that they moved when I pointed them at the television. The rods kept moving during the afternoon whenever I would either point them at the rocking chair or the television. They did not move when pointed anywhere else in the house. Finally, at 3:30 PM the rods stopped moving when pointed at the rocking chair or the television. They had moved when pointed at either of those objects during a number of trials that I made over a stretch of time covering two hours and fifteen minutes, and they have never moved since that day when I have pointed them at the chair or the television.

For some time I thought it was odd the rods would move only when pointed at the chair and the TV, and not when pointed at anything else in the house. Then, I was suddenly struck by the thought that a spirit could be sitting in the chair and psychically watching the television. My father, who died in 1981, used to sit in that chair and watch television!

I told Tom about the various hard-to-explain incidents that had happened at my home, and he said, "They know you are looking for hard evidence, and they are giving it to you." On November 20, 1999, Tom came to my home to see if it was haunted. After he entered the house, he quickly walked through it and went into the back room. He looked at a chair which is close to my bed and which faces it, and said that somebody sits in that chair at night and watches me. He said it is a man, shorter than I am but more heavy set. That description fits my father. He said that the man had done a lot of work on our property. My father had spent much of his life working in our grove. Without knowing what my father looked like or what he did, he said he picked up the word "father."

At one point Tom sat in the chair and hooked up a galvanic meter to his skin. He took out a ouija board he had brought with him, and the galvanic meter started to make a clicking noise. Tom said the static noise speeds up if a spirit comes near him. The machine was just clicking a little bit at first, but it kept going faster and faster until it was screaming like a model airplane engine. Tom said that the spirit was trying to come through. He said, "Calm down. Stop it! Stop it! I will not use this if you don't calm down." The furious static noise gradually slowed down over a period of minutes, until it had almost stopped. Then the ouija board began to spell out a message. He never looked at the board as he moved the pointer that came to rest on each letter. It spelled out "dad." Tom asked if it was John's dad and it spelled out "yes." Then the ouija board spelled "John." After it spelled "ash" and "aka" and a few additional garbled combinations of letters, he stopped using the board. He said, "Maybe it is your father, or it could just be spirits playing tricks." Tom asked if my father had been cremated. When I said yes, Tom speculated that this could be the reason that ash had been spelled. He guessed that aka might signify "also known as John's dad," which he thought might be a little ghostly attempt at humor.

Then we heard a noise a few feet to the north of us that sounded like a single rap on the wall made by someone's knuckles. We both looked out the window to see if my mother had been outside the room and had made a bumping noise against the outside wall, but there was nobody there.

Tom then pulled out a pendulum and said we would use it to get some answers. He said that the pendulum supposedly draws on universal knowledge. The pendulum had a clear crystalline ball dangling from a metal chain. Tom placed a chart under it which showed that a movement toward and away from the holder meant yes, a movement from side to side in front of the holder meant no, and a circular motion meant that it didn't know. Tom placed both of his elbows on a flat surface, held the pendulum with two fingers of one hand, and steadied those two fingers with two fingers of the other hand. After he asked a question, the pendulum would start to swing vigorously in one direction or another, despite the fact that his hands and fingers were motionless.

Tom asked, "Is this house occupied by a spirit entity?" The pendulum's clear movement from side to side in front of Tom gave a negative reply. Tom then asked, "Does a spirit entity come to visit?" This time the pendulum started swinging toward and away from Tom and the answer was yes. Tom asked if the pendulum could tell us who it was that visited, and it again showed a yes answer. Tom said, "Is this spirit related to John?" The answer was yes. Tom asked, "Is it John's father?" Once again the answer was yes.

Tom then handed the pendulum to me. After he showed me how to hold it, I asked, "Is my dad here?" I held my hands as still as I possibly could, and was astounded to see the pendulum start to swing in a direction toward and away from me indicating an answer of yes. Tom asked, "Did John's father make the noise against the wall?" The pendulum answered yes. I asked, "Do you have a message you want to give us?" There was no movement.

Tom said he had never visited a house where he asked a spirit if it was living there and it said no. He said when he visited a house and communicated with a spirit, the answer had always been yes before. He said that the answer was so unusual that he thought it must be true.

Do I accept the answers that the pendulum gave as the truth? When he finished investigating our house, Tom gave the pendulum to me. I have made much use of it since that day, and found that some of its answers turn out to be incorrect. When I ask if its answers are always correct, it answers no. Tom said he gave it to me, not because it is infallibly accurate, but because it will help show me there is another side.

I have found the pendulum to be capricious, surprising, very unpredictable, and fascinating. At first it would only answer a few of my questions, and then later it started answering all of them. It even answered questions about some of the greatest mysteries of all time, such as the following examples. Did Lee Harvey Oswald act alone in assassinating John F. Kennedy? Did George Leigh-Mallory and Andrew Irvine reach the top of Mt. Everest before falling to their deaths on the way down in 1924? Does intelligent life exist on other planets in the universe? According to the pendulum, Lee Harvey Oswald did act alone, Leigh-Mallory and Irvine did not reach the summit, and intelligent life exists only on Earth.

The pendulum would answer all of my questions with the same answer on a given day, even when I repeated questions a number of times. However, on another day, it would give different answers to some of those same questions. Still later, its answers became more consistent from one day to another. Initially it would not answer my mother's questions when she tried using it. She asked if it would answer her questions and it answered no. She asked if it liked her and it again answered no. My brother and sister-in-law came for a visit, and it didn't answer my sister-in-law's questions when she tried using it. I asked it if it would answer my brother's questions, and it answered no. Later, it decided it liked my mother, and began to answer her questions.

Sometimes the pendulum would not move at all in response to my questions on a certain day, but, then, it would answer my questions again the next day. In February 2000, it would not move at all in response to my questions for four consecutive days. I kept asking all sorts of questions, but it remained motionless. During the same stretch of time, my mother tried it, and it answered her questions with vigorous movements. On the fifth day, it still didn't answer my questions. Finally, I asked it, "Are you refusing to answer my questions to show me that the answers are coming from the other side and not just from the movements of my hands?" Then came an answer---yes! After that, it began to answer all of my questions again.

I had pretty much decided there really wasn't anything to the pendulum's answers before this happened, and its failure to answer questions for several days made me take it much more seriously. Even though it felt as though the pendulum was moving on its own, prior to the stretch of time when it wouldn't answer anything, I had the feeling that some motion of my hands must be making it move. After spending several days asking countless questions without ever seeing any movement, I decided that something else must move it than the movements of my fingers and hands.

The pendulum also answered all of my questions about the ghosts in the old church. It answered that Kristina had come to our house in the past, but stated that none of the other church ghosts had done so. It replied that Kristina had been released from the church. It gave yes answers to my questions about whether many of the ghosts that have been reported are actually in the church. These ghosts include the lady in the pantry, the lady who sits in a pew near the front of the church, and the lady who sits in a pew at the back of the church. It also answered affirmatively to the presence of the gnome who spends his time on the stairway and in the broom closet at the top of the stairway, and the ghost in the groom's room.

The pendulum concluded that the ghost in the groom's room is a short man and not a boy. The pendulum also replied that the homeless ghosts and the ghost that Tom called Charles had all left the pantry and the church. The pendulum has given consistent answers to all of these questions about the ghosts in the church when asked repeatedly over a period of time.

Everyone who has tried the pendulum feels that it moves by itself, and not because of any motions of their hands. It often delays for a short time when you ask it a question, and then you can see it suddenly change its direction of motion when it gives its answer. When it gives an unexpected answer or one you strongly disagree with, you definitely get the feeling that it is moving on its own, and not in response to some subconscious movements of your hands.

Even though I have learned to regard the pendulum with amazement, I can't take its answers as certain, including the one that my father comes to visit. If his spirit does come to the house, it would be in character for him to play some of the tricks that have happened. He loved pranks, and I am sure that he would try to convince us that there is survival after death. He made a pact with a friend of his that whoever died first would try to come back and get a message to the survivor. My father's friend died first, and my father said that he had not received any sign from his deceased friend. If he visits the house, he might be trying to show us that there is an existence beyond death.

Tom told me about another use of the pendulum that I experimented with and found somewhat unsettling when I tried it in our house. He said that if you hold it near a ghost it begins to rotate in a counterclockwise direction. I went around using the pendulum in various locations in the house after he had left, and found that it spun very impressively in a counterclockwise motion when I held it over the chair by my bed, but it did not rotate anywhere else in the house. Nearly every time since that I have walked all over the house looking for places where it would spin counterclockwise, I have found that it does it in just one location. This might be on a chair or sofa, in a doorway, or in the middle of a room. It seemed like it was finding the place where the spirit was at that moment.

Once, the pendulum spun counterclockwise in two locations while I was walking through the house doing my investigation, as though the spirit had moved from one place to another. In rare cases, I can't find anyplace in the house where it will rotate. I also tried it in our adjacent rental house, which had originally belonged to my grandparents, and I found a spot in that house where the pendulum began to rotate ominously in a counterclockwise rotation. Was there a ghost in that house also? In addition I found that the pendulum did its spin in places where Tom, Jan, or Denise had pointed out ghosts in the church. Almost always the rotation was counterclockwise, although on a couple of occasions it went clockwise. The pendulum, unlike the dowsing rods that usually don't even move for me, seems to be extremely good at locating ghosts for someone who has little or no psychic ability.

During Tom's visit on November 20, 1999, he noticed an area in our orchard where he felt some supernatural activity. He said that he had the impression that there had once been something like a town meeting in that location. I have no information that such an event ever took place, but I don't know what happened on our property before my grandfather planted the grove in 1907.

18   Mysterious Movements

After Tom's visit, strange things continued to happen in my house. In early September 2000, I began to find dried cat food in places where I would never expect to see it. The cat food is kept in a bowl on the kitchen floor where the cats have easy access to it. It has been there for many years without ever showing up anywhere else in the house. But it turned up on top of my bed, on a rug by my bed, on a rug on my bathroom floor, on a window ledge by the toothpaste tube in my bathroom, and, on three different occasions, in one of the cuffs of my jeans. When the dried cat food appeared in my pants cuff there were lots of pieces of it---eight or ten or more on each occasion.

When I lift up a bowl and place cat food in it, I occasionally spill some. I tried spilling it down my pants to see if any would go into my cuffs. Despite repeated trials not one particle of the dried cat food ever wound up in my cuff. When I looked at the cuffs I could see why---they were too tight against the pants and there were folds of cloth just above them. The only person around who could have put cat food into my cuffs was my mother, and that idea is ludicrous. She never plays pranks, doesn't tell lies, and tries her best to keep me from finding evidence of ghosts to talk and write about. She says that she couldn't stand to live in a house with a ghost, and doesn't like me telling others that our house is haunted. She even kept her story of hearing a little girl's footsteps from me for a long time. She would never provide me with evidence to tell people that our house has a ghost in it. Since that week in September 2000 I have never again seen cat food outside the kitchen.

I also saw one of the cats get an invisible helping hand to get outside the house. The cat was sitting by the front door waiting to get out. The wooden door was open, and the screen door was closed. Suddenly, I saw the screen door flung wide open, just as if a person had done it, and the cat walked out. There was no breeze that would have caused this to happen.

A few weeks later I was eating one of my mother's home made cookies. I was shocked to find a piece of glass in it. The next night I was eating another one and found another piece of glass. My mother thought that there might be some little pieces of sand in the cookies that I was mistaking for glass. Then she ate one and found a piece of glass in it. I kept this square piece of clear glass. It is about 3/8 inch long and wide, and about 1/8 inch thick. I thoroughly checked the flour jar, sugar jar, and container of preserved fruit fragments that she had used as ingredients for the cookies. There was not a trace of glass anywhere. Needless to say, this was the first batch of cookies my mother ever made that contained fragments of glass. This certainly was not a prank that my father would have played on us. Maybe it was the shady character from the groom's room or the gnome that some people said is often on the stairs in the church.

I met Tom and talked with him about the series of strange incidents. Tom said that when I focused so much on ghosts, I noticed more ghostly things (like when you learn about something and then suddenly you hear about it and read about it everywhere). Then when the ghosts saw that I noticed them, they began to flock to me. Tom said that was why things were happening to me. He told me that if others would focus on ghosts like I did, they would have more experiences too. Tom said he thought that ghosts other than my dad had come to visit my house.

One could easily become so paranoid about ghosts that any strange incident could be attributed to them. On June 7, 2000, for example, Jean came for a visit, and was talking with my mother about her new clothes dryer. My mother had always hung her clothes on a clothesline to dry and found it hard to make herself use the new machine. Jean said that she needed to use her new dryer, and then drove off a few minutes later in her car. Shortly after Jean left I heard a tremendous crash out back of the house. An enormous branch had fallen from a huge mimosa tree, landed directly on top of the clothesline, and knocked it flat onto the ground.

Another odd incident took place in May 2001. Jean had to be at a hospital early that morning to have surgery. I told her I would drive her to the hospital. When I got to her house I discovered that my watch

126

was ten minutes faster than the clock in my car. The clock in my car had agreed with the clock at my home, so I hoped that my watch was wrong. When we arrived at the hospital we discovered that my watch was ten minutes fast.

My watch was relatively new and it had always kept very accurate time. I had used it the day before and it was accurate then. It has kept very accurate time every since the trip to the hospital on May 29. Why had it gained ten minutes on the morning of Jean's operation? I know that I had not reset it deliberately or by accident, since it is not simple to change the time on it - it couldn't happen just by brushing against it. I joked with Jean that her late husband had set it ahead ten minutes to make certain that I would get her to the hospital on time.

My mother always tried to come up with some explanation for the strange things that had happened in our home. In October 2001 something happened that she said she could not explain away. There is a chair in the living room just to the west of the entrance to the kitchen. We generally stack letters to be mailed on the eastern-most arm of the chair. One evening she had stacked three letters on this chair-arm and next morning we both noticed that the letters were gone. She said, "Good, you have mailed the letters already," but I had not. I looked around and saw all three stacked neatly on end together against the wall and behind the leg of an antique cabinet that sits to the west of the chair by the entrance.

Neither of us had placed them there, and they could not have fallen to that position from their location on the arm of the chair. There was just no way they could been moved to that location, but it had happened. This finally convinced her beyond a doubt of the existence of the spirit world. My mother, who used to think that there is no survival of death, now knows otherwise. She is only one of a series of people whose outlooks have been changed by the ghostly incidents with which I have been connected. People mentioned in the previous chapters, like Connie, Wes, and Cheryl, who came to the church hoping for an experience with a ghost, remain impressed by their encounters with the supernatural. A half dozen atheists and agnostics who are long-time friends of mine and who have never had an experience in the old church now admit that they are far less confident

127

of their beliefs, or lack of same, after hearing my accounts. My brother, a Stanford engineering professor and his wife, both longtime skeptics about life-after-death, and my nephews, far more inclined to believe, all show varying degrees of being impressed by the ghost stories.

My mother was also amazed by a couple of other apparently impossible movements of objects. One day she went into the front room of our three-room storeroom, looked down at the floor, and saw an old-fashioned, flower-shaped glass button from one of her mother's dresses. It had been in a box that was kept in the storeroom, and she couldn't imagine how it had come to rest on the rug. We go into the front section of the storeroom every day, and the button had not been on the floor before. Nobody had opened the box since she put it in the storeroom. Someone asked her what she thought when she saw it, and she said she felt like saying, "Hi, mom."

Then our faithful old pruning saw that I lost over a year before turned up in its customary place in our gun closet. On Monday, Nov. 25, 2002, a roaring north wind broke a large branch from a silver maple tree in our yard, and dropped it onto a telephone line and two electric wires. I rushed into the house to get a pruning saw, hoping to cut the limb to pieces before its massive weight caused the wires to break. When I reached the gun cabinet in my mother's closet where we normally keep our pruning saw, I expected to see a folding pruning saw. This saw was a replacement for the better saw that my family had used for decades until I lost it. I had forgotten that the folding saw was not now in the gun cabinet, but was in the back bedroom of the house where I had left it. Instead, to my astonishment, there was our old pruning saw in the gun cabinet. I had laid it down outdoors after cutting off some limbs one day and never could find it again, despite hours of searching. I figured it might have been hauled away with all the branches that were taken to the dump.

This venerable old saw had not been in the gun cabinet when I took the folding saw from it a few weeks earlier. There were only a couple of other people who knew that we kept a saw there, and they had not been in our house since long before I last took the folding saw out of the cabinet. Nobody else had been in my mother's closet who could have put the saw there. The old saw was in as good a condition as it had been when I last saw it. It was simply impossible for it to be there, but there it was.

A skeptic might say that these incidents don't show conclusively that a ghost moved the objects since I can't prove there was nobody who moved them when I was not watching. I did see an object actually moved without any visible agent to move it, however, on one occasion. I was getting ready to eat dinner and had just poured myself a glass of grape juice and placed it to the right of my plate a few inches from the edge of the table. I briefly left to do something else and then returned to the table and sat down to eat. I was puzzled to see no drink by my plate since I was sure I had just put it there. I looked all over the house for the drink to see if I had set it down somewhere absentmindedly. I couldn't see it anywhere. I even passed by the table a couple of times and looked all over the table to make sure it wasn't there. I told my mom I couldn't find my drink and she looked at the table and saw that it wasn't there.

Finally, I poured myself another grape drink and placed it just to the right of my plate. After I sat down I saw only my second drink, but then I was suddenly amazed to see two drinks side by side just to the right of my plate. I am certain there was no glass of grape juice there when I first sat down to dinner or when I put the second glass of juice by my plate. I was looking toward my second glass of juice when I saw the first one I had poured instantly appear out of nothingness. Tom has said that one of signs that a ghost is present is to have something disappear and then reappear. He told me he had once had his glasses disappear, then bought a new pair, only to find the first pair again in the same place he always kept them. Did my mom think I was crazy? To my surprise she said she totally believed me when I said the glass had disappeared and then reappeared.

I had wondered how it would look to see a ghost moving something. Would the thing being moved appear to float through the air by itself? The drinking glass instantly materialized out of nothing. Perhaps it dematerialized and then materialized, and did not actually move as a solid object in the space between. This is called teleportation, and the object moved is called an apport. The same thing appeared to have happened when I asked a ghost to play a trick on Tom and a penny seemed to instantly materialize out of nothing in front of the groom's room chair and footstool. This could also explain how a solid object, such as the pruning saw, could come into the house from outdoors when there was no opening into the house.

Teleportation is often reported to occur during a poltergeist episode. Did we have a poltergeist or was my dad trying to show he is still here? I can't say with any certainty. We certainly didn't have a young girl or boy living with us of the type often reported to be associated with poltergeist activity.

How could one possibly explain the dematerialization and materialization of the drinking glass? Could there be a physical explanation or would nothing short of real magic do it? A first-rate Stanford University physicist named Dr. William A. Tiller has speculated about how this might happen. My brother, Dr. James L. Adams, a professor of engineering at Stanford University for 30 years until his retirement, told me that Tiller was sent to the Soviet Union to evaluate research in parapsychology. Much to the shock of Stanford University, he concluded that there was something to it.

Then, in the 1960s, Tiller decided to work on paranormal topics in addition to his main work as a professor in the Department of Materials Science at Stanford University. Tiller spent over 30 years in Stanford's Department of Materials Science, served for years as chairman of the department, and was and is widely recognized as one of the world's leading scientists on the structure of matter. Tiller's theories of the paranormal have predictably drawn scoffing in contrast to the great respect shown for his work in materials science, but they are ingenious and interesting. He proposed a theory of two realities in a mirror type relationship, the first one being the familiar physical world made up of electric matter of positive mass traveling at speeds less than the speed of light. He calls the other reality the etheric matter world and speculates that it is made up of magnetic matter of negative mass traveling faster than the speed of light. His ideas about this unseen reality are based on considerations of the nature of the vacuum of space. Tiller stated in his 1997 book, Science and Human Transformation, that his theory shows "a possible structure of the universe which would allow new classes of phenomena to exist in the universe and be as valid as those perceived by our five physical senses but not be directly perceivable by that limited set of senses."

Tiller said that an object might be dematerialized by moving it to a higher dimensional space (some theories of physics have proposed that space has as many as 26 dimensions) and transferring it into the postulated etheric matter world. Materializing it would be done by the reversal of this process. He posits a particle called a deltron that would facilitate movement between the two separated realities. Maybe this will be established science in a century or two, although it can only be regarded as clever speculation at present.

I once saw another example of what might have been teleportation, and it was so astounding I still have trouble believing it even though I saw it with my own eyes. It made me wonder if it would it be possible to make a solid object materialize inside another solid object rather than in empty space.

I was taking off my shoes one evening, and suddenly the right side of the shoelace on my right shoe snapped, and came off in my fingers. I said, "OOOOOOOOOOOH!" I was disgusted that I would have to find another shoelace and replace the broken one. I placed the shoe on the floor with the broken shoelace immediately beside it. I asked my mother, who was seated a short distance away, where the spare shoelaces were. Then I looked down at the shoe again, and was dumbfounded to see that the shoelace was not broken at all, but was completely intact. I might have convinced myself that I just imagined the shoelace breaking, but when I told my mother what had happened she said that she had heard a snapping sound, like a breaking shoelace would have made, just before she heard me say, "OOOOOOOOOOOH!" When I talked to Tom about this incident later, I said that I couldn't tell other people about it or write about it because they would think I am crazy, and he said, "Go ahead and write about it. They will think you are crazy anyway."

Could the broken shoelace have been dematerialized when I took my eyes off it for an instant, and then materialized so that the broken end of the loose piece of shoelace reappeared inside the broken end of the shoelace still on the shoe? Could this then have made an instant and neat rejoining of the fragmented pieces?

In November 2001, I had a very spooky experience while I was lying on a sofa in our front room. It was 6:45 PM and dark outside. I was reading, and I heard the sound of a loud footstep as if someone had stepped up onto the concrete front porch. This porch is very visible from the front room through large windows, and the porch light was on. I looked to see who it was, and I saw an extremely blurry-looking, ill-defined form (no outline of a body showing) moving at the pace of a walk across the front porch. It looked like the image I had seen in the naugahyde chair of the groom's room in January 1999. It was translucent, it obscured objects behind it, and it was of man-sized height and width. Could it have been the ghost from the groom's room, or was it my dad or another spirit? I don't expect to ever know for sure.

Most of my spooky encounters have caused me to feel fascinated rather than frightened, but this one really gave me the creeps. I was shaking for a couple of minutes. As time passed I didn't notice anything else unusual, however, and I eventually returned to a calm state of mind.

There was another strange incident at my house when I returned from my high school class reunion at 9:50 PM in June 2002. My mother said one of the cats seemed to hear me when I drove in. Then she heard four little knocks on our back door. An instant later I came in the front door. She had wondered why I would knock on the back door. I didn't. I said, "It was a ghost."

In December 2002 my mother was in our back bedroom when she heard two heavy footsteps directly behind her. She looked around the house to see if I could have made the sounds and saw that I was reclining on a sofa in the front room. She told me that she had always expected that it would be very frightening to have a ghost in the house, but it was not. She said that having experiences such as hearing the footsteps seemed very matter of fact. Another time I heard footsteps approaching me from behind my computer chair, and then I felt a hand touch my back. There was nobody behind me.

Skeptics might say that she had been influenced by my talk of a ghost, heard some of the usual creaking noises that can be noticed in any old house, and concluded that it was the footsteps of a ghost. I am sure this is not true because she can easily tell the difference between the sounds of footsteps and the creaking sounds of a house. She stepped on the floor a couple of times when she told me the story to demonstrate the sounds that she heard. About the same time another experience took place that could not possibly be explained away in such a manner. I was walking toward the kitchen from the back bedroom where I had been talking with my mother when I heard someone whistling in our house. I heard her alarmed voice say, "Did you hear someone whistle?" She said the sound of the whistling, which was like someone trying to get another person's attention, came a few feet away from her near the pillow of my bed. It was around 11:40 AM on a cold, rainy morning, and all the windows and doors were closed. There was nobody close by outside of the house, no one else inside, and there is no way that anyone can mistake a clear sound from inside the house with the muffled sounds that come from outside. It was also clearly the sound of someone whistling, and not a sound that could be confused with any inanimate sound such as the whistling of a teakettle. There was no kettle heating on the stove, no strong wind blowing, nor any other condition or implement that could have caused a whistling sound.

19 Cathy

Jan Hagman called me to say she wanted to have a tea for a group of women in the old church during which she and her guests would discuss reincarnation. Tom would be there to help her set up everything. I told her this sounded like a great idea, and I said I also hoped she and Tom would have some time to do a little investigating of the ghosts in the church. Jan said she thought they would able to do that.

The tea was scheduled for June 30, 2001. Tom had time to do some looking around the church that afternoon while the tea was going on downstairs. In the front of the sanctuary just below the stage where the piano sits, Tom said he saw the ghost of a girl about nine or ten years old with sandy hair and wearing a pinafore dress. Tom said she was not Kristina. She was leading a procession of boys and girls who looked like they could have been in costume for some sort of performance. He said one of the girls had a little Dutch girl hat. Tom said the girl in the pinafore dress was the most conspicuous of the children. As the children neared the stage, Tom told me they suddenly faded out. Tom said he wished someone else could corroborate what he had seen.

After Tom had his vision of the little girl in the pinafore dress apparently taking part in a performance along with other ghost children, he had expressed a wish for somebody else to confirm this. A couple of weeks later his wish came true.

On July 14, 2001 Denise came to the church with her daughter, Cathy Mancini. Denise had told me about her daughter's abilities to sense ghosts. All three of her daughters are in her opinion sensitive to the spirit world, but Cathy's powers are the strongest. Denise said Cathy's abilities are much stronger than her own powers. She believes Cathy is almost a shaman. Cathy works as a highly skilled microbiologist and chemist in an environmental laboratory, but her unearthly abilities allow her to do things that other microbiologists couldn't imagine possible. She can often predict calamities in addition to observing ghosts.

Denise said Cathy once had a very bad feeling when her sister was leaving on an automobile trip, and warned her not to go. Her sister heeded this advice, as her sisters always do when she asks them not to do something. There was an accident and four people in the car were killed. Another time Cathy was taking food to her husband, who was a deputy in a courtroom. She knew the judge and commented to him that the defendant would soon be dead. Other inmates killed the man shortly afterward.

Denise said that on another occasion she was going into a restaurant with Cathy and another of her daughters and Cathy said, "Don't go in here. Let's leave!" The other daughter agreed with Cathy. Denise was going to protest, but then they left. Later they learned the place was robbed ten minutes after they left, and everyone was forced to lie on the floor. Another time Cathy felt that one of her sisters had been in an accident, and when she called her sister, she learned it had been true.

Cathy and Denise have even had simultaneous and identical dreams or visions. Denise had a near-death experience in a hospital and saw her deceased son standing in the corner of a hospital room. Later she learned that Cathy, while at home, had the same vision of her brother standing in the corner of a hospital room at the same time. In this double vision, Cathy told her brother, "She's not ready to go yet!" Her brother shrugged his shoulders and disappeared.

Denise and Cathy are very hesitant to tell people about their experiences for fear of being thought crazy, whereas their psychic Cherokee Indian ancestors were greatly respected by members of their tribe for their abilities and were sought out for advice. Denise told me that when people died they appeared to Cathy's great grandmother in her dreams to show they were gone. She lived on low ground near the Mississippi River and closed and opened homes for rich people in that area when they vacationed in Europe. Once, she got a message to open a home for a couple, and she didn't do it. She was told she had better open the home, but she said she would not because the woman had appeared to her in a dream and she knew the woman was dead. A couple of days later a telegram arrived which instructed her not to open the home because the woman had died.

Denise told me that Cathy's grandmother also had extraordinary abilities. For example, she could find anything that was lost. She would occasionally write to Denise and tell her where to find things that Denise had lost, even though Denise hadn't even told her that she had lost them yet. The uncanny abilities were passed down through the generations and Cathy's teenage daughter, Carla, is now developing her own powers.

Cathy is an impressive person for reasons other than her psychic powers. Over a period of time I would discover that Cathy is generous, adventurous, intelligent, has a powerful memory, and knows a surprisingly large amount about a long list of subjects. In addition to her fascination with the paranormal, she has wide-ranging interests in many things that are artistic or scientific. She loves to draw, write, sew, and do most anything else that is creative, and she also enjoys her work in the lab. She loves to read books about a wide variety of topics. She has had an uncommonly broad education, including a BS in medical microbiology with a chemistry minor from California State University at Long Beach, a BS in psychology with a criminal justice minor from California State University at Fullerton, and she also graduated from the Sheriff's Academy. She was formerly employed as a clerk and then a deputy in the Orange County Sheriff's Department. She worked in the county jail when she was a deputy.

After having heard the stories about Cathy's psychic capabilities and unusual background, I was excited as I waited for Denise and Cathy to arrive at the church. Denise said she had told Cathy nothing about the ghosts in the church, except to say that the church was haunted and that she had sensed the presence of a little girl. After hearing about the girl ghost, Cathy told Denise the ghost was there because her ashes are kept in the church. Denise told me that at the time Cathy told this to her, Denise had not yet learned from Elizabeth that Kristina's ashes are in the church and Cathy did not know it either. Denise said she had kept her knowledge of the church ghosts from Cathy because she was looking forward to having her come to the church and wanted to see what she would conclude on her own. Denise was not aware of many details of other people's experiences in the church that had taken place when she was not there, so she could not have told Cathy those things even if she had wanted to. Cathy had never met Tom or any of the people who help him investigate haunted buildings.

I saw Denise and Cathy turn into the lot behind the church at 10 AM and the car traveled erratically past the parking spaces. Cathy then backed up and turned her car toward the church to park. When she got out of her car, I saw a very attractive young woman with shimmering black hair, piercing eyes, and an armload of jingling silver bracelets. She was dressed in black, and there was something about her appearance that seemed very unique and mystical. She displayed a vibrant personality, and was very intense and very serious. She was later to say that she had driven so erratically into the parking lot because she was overcome by an overpowering feeling of sadness as she turned into the lot.

Cathy first went into the museum building north of the church. She said the feeling of sadness was so strong it was like being on the receiving end of a violent punch when she walked into the museum. She had a terrible feeling of despondency in the room filled with old clothes and in the restroom. It was so bad she burst into tears. A lady's corset was part of the decorations hanging on the bathroom wall, and the corset gave her a bad feeling. Elizabeth later told us that the corset had belonged to her mother-in-law, and she added that this woman was very domineering. Jean said she heard Cathy say she saw the ghost of a woman walking down the hallway of the museum.

Most of the ghosts have been reported in the old church, but there have also been some ghosts observed in the museum building. Elizabeth and I heard a disembodied voice coming from the hallway as we sat in the den of the museum. A boy touring with a third grade class told me that he had seen the ghost of a woman in the museum building. Betty, the ghost-sensing card player who had observed Kristina before Denise joined the card games, said Kristina liked to play in the clothes room in the museum. Julia, my nephew's girl friend, had strong movements of the dowsing rods when she pointed them in the clothes room.

Cathy, Denise, and I then left the museum building and headed for the door on the south side of the church. After we walked into the sanctuary, Cathy said she saw the ghost of a girl who was around eight or nine years old that looked like somebody from the 1930s, although she was dressed as somebody in an earlier time. She looked as though she was taking part in a play or pageant. She had on a light blue long sleeved dress like a prairie dress, and was wearing a full-length apron. The apron had a front bib that covered the dress, and it had a bow in back. She described the girl's hair as light colored and said it was pulled back. Like Tom, she said that other children were taking part in the performance but the little girl stood out the most. She also said there were several women ghosts in the pews watching the performance.

The little girl in the dress and full-length apron was standing just in front of the center of the stage at the front of the sanctuary. As we walked across the stage Cathy said she could see the children giving the performance standing all around us and they were completely unaware of our presence. Being among the children with them unaware of her reminded her of dreams of going to school naked and having nobody notice.

I was astounded to hear the close agreement between what Cathy said and what Tom had told me two weeks before. He told of a girl 9 or 10 with sandy hair, wearing a pinafore dress, and taking part in a performance with other less conspicuous children. Cathy told of a girl 8 or 9 with light hair, wearing a pinafore dress, and taking part in a performance with other less conspicuous children. Cathy could not have known what Tom had told me so the agreement is incredible. When I told Tom about this later, he said, "I wished for someone to corroborate what I said, and it happened. Now I should wish to win the lottery."

Cathy said both the church and museum are portals and she felt like she was going to be sucked in. She said a lot of the ghosts were connected with the church during their lifetimes, but the portal lets in many other entities that need help. They can't get help in their own places so they go elsewhere to get it. She said only a select few portals exist. Most haunted sites are not connected with portals. Tom had also said he feels the church is a portal, and believes spirits may come to the church from other places because they feel they can get help to be released. This may have happened because of all the spirit communications held in the church. Tom said Kristina might be telling trapped ghosts of children to go to the church where a man will help them to go on their way.

We began to walk toward the hallway behind the sanctuary, and I was anxiously waiting to see what Cathy would say when she got to the groom's room. She passed the piano on the stage and said she felt a chilly spot. Many people have reported a cold spot by the piano although there is no evidence of an unusual draft there. We walked into the hallway leading to the groom's room and bride's room, and Cathy said it was freezing. She started crying. When I unlocked the door to the groom's room, she shuddered and said to whomever was in the groom's room, "See ya!" She said, "It is really oppressive in here." I asked Cathy who was in the room, and she said, "He's a monster." She estimated his height at about 5 feet 10 inches, and said he had dark brown hair. She said he reminded her of a man in a small town who would give you the creeps – perhaps Billy Bob Thornton in some of his movie parts. Later I mentioned to Cathy that many other people had described the ghost in the groom's room as short, and she said, "I saw him sitting. Maybe they saw him standing."

Cathy said he was a bad person who had done something and never atoned for it. She told us he was not restricted to this room. She said he thinks he has power but he doesn't. He uses the unknown to make people feel bad. She said he is angry, but she had no impression he was sorry for anything he had done. She felt he was tired and wanted to leave

Denise used to feel a headache when she walked down the hallway toward the groom's room, but she had not suffered one the last few times she had come to the groom's room. She had hoped the man she sensed there was gone. This time Denise said she had felt her headache again when she walked down the hallway. Cathy said he was still there but he could go into the wall to convince you he was gone. She also said that this was the man who held the south church door shut on earlier occasions when we tried to enter it

Cathy called him a 1920s or 30s drifter type, although she also got an impression of the 1940s. She told me that he had murdered someone in a house and someone else in another place. He raped and murdered a woman because she rebuffed him. Cathy said he can't leave the church building, but he can go anywhere in the church except for the bride's room. She said, "He looks at himself in the mirror, sees his true self, and doesn't like it. His anger won't allow him to feel sorry for what he has done, and he can't help himself. Someone has to help him before he can atone, and no one wants to help him. It is the perfect punishment for him. He could suck in a weak person without protection. He could get into their mind, read their thoughts, encourage them to do something wrong, or take away their feelings of guilt about something they had done that was wrong."

There had been differing reports from various people about whether there was a malicious man or a mischievous boy in the groom's room, but Cathy was to tell me later that both were in the building. The ghost of the man who was frequently encountered in the groom's room was not always there, and sometimes other ghosts, such as the boy, entered the room.

We left the groom's room behind and walked into the bride's room. Cathy said she had "no bad vibes" in this room. Cathy said the rapist-murderer ghost can't come into the bride's room, and other spirits come into the room to avoid him and to look at themselves in the many mirrors on the wall.

When we came out of the bride's room we heard someone knocking on the nearby south church door. I heard a man's voice speaking. We opened the door and nobody was there. There was nobody anywhere else in sight outside the building. Was it the man from the groom's room?

We walked down the stairs toward the church basement. Cathy said a mischievous little boy likes to hang out on the stairs to tease people and grab them around the leg. Previously Denise had had a mysterious mark on the side of her leg by her knee, and told Cathy about it. Cathy asked, "Did you go to the church?" Denise replied she had, and Cathy said the boy had caused it by kissing her knee. The mark had disappeared by the time Cathy came to tour the church. Cathy had told Denise about the boy on the stairs before ever touring the church or having been told any stories about the ghosts.

We next went into the kitchen area. Cathy said there was a lot of agitation in the kitchen. She had a feeling of overwhelming sadness in the kitchen. She went into the pantry and said she felt an oppressive feeling, but added that she was not being told to leave. There was a woman ghost in the pantry who gave out the message, "I will share with you but don't trespass on my space."

She said this ghost was in the leadership role of a head cook. She described her as follows: "She is in a 1940s dress, with her hair pulled back in a bun. She has salt and pepper hair. She is forty-five to fifty-five. She is a lady of substance built like a brick shanty. She is not obese, but stout." I told Cathy that Tom had described a very similar woman in the pantry during our Halloween spirit communication in 1997 and said she had a Germanic look. She excitedly said, "That's exactly right. She does have a Germanic look."

She went on to say, "The cook lady knows something. She knows what went on, maybe as a witness or having read about it in the newspaper, and she wants to tell someone. The crime took place in a secluded utilitarian type room off a bed chamber. She's talking about the murderer in the groom's room. She wishes he had been caught. He's so smug. He should have been caught but the police couldn't put two and two together. She doesn't want to leave until the truth is known. That's her purpose---not today but teleporting back to then and playing out what should have happened."

Now Cathy was heading into the hallway north of the kitchen. I watched closely as Cathy started to open the door to the storeroom that has always given Tom and Denise such a feeling of horror. She peered into the room and her face instantly contorted with shock and horror. She said, "It looks like the room where the lady was murdered." She instantly shut the door, pulled back, and broke into tears.

Cathy said it was like seeing a movie when she opened the door to the storeroom. At first she thought the woman had been strangled, but she saw blood and figured the man may have hit her on the head too. Cathy said the woman was not very big, and was easily overpowered. He approached her from the back and she had no chance. She had very delicate features, was in good health, and was very beautiful. She was interested in someone else and not the drifter

141

character. Cathy said she had the impression the lady was not actually murdered in the storeroom, but felt that this ghostly crime scene could only materialize in a place that is extremely similar to where the crime took place. The storeroom in the church had originally been a coal storage room for the boiler.

Cathy felt that the lady in the pantry was working for a family, and the murderer was hired to work where his victim was living. She thought that somebody had connected him to the murder but there was not enough evidence to convict him. She sensed that he didn't live to be terribly old, but she also had the impression that another person hadn't killed him. She thought he drank too much and died of carelessness, such as in a fall or in an automobile accident. Cathy thought people had been relieved when he died. He had terrorized certain people in town and many thought his death to be too normal compared to what he deserved.

Cathy had described the ghosts in the church in extraordinary detail. She said when she is in a haunted location the ghosts appear as lifelike to her as if they were living people. After Cathy had finished her examination of all parts of the museum and church, I thanked her and Denise for a fascinating time. I was already making plans in my mind to arrange for Tom, Jan, Cathy, Denise, and I to explore the church together as soon as possible. There was such a mounting pile of agreement that perhaps we were approaching an answer as to who was haunting the church and why.

20   A Ghost with a Message

I arranged for Cathy, Denise, and Tom to come to the church on a Saturday morning, in August 2001. Cathy and Tom had never met before. I was intensely curious to see if Tom and Cathy would make the same observations of ghosts that day, or if they would disagree. Tom has said that a lot of what you see depends on the rapport you have with what is on the other side.

Jan was unable to come because she had to work. Denise and Cathy arrived before Tom, and the three of us entered the church at 10:20 AM. I wondered if Cathy would still sense the children's group performing in the front of the sanctuary. When we walked into the sanctuary Cathy said the children are always there, and the performance seems to go on forever, but to the participants the duration of time is probably like the blink of an eye.

Denise had the impression that something had just happened that was causing quite a stir among the ghosts. She said it was like people had just found out news at an old fashioned town meeting. She sensed a lot of movement and milling around. Cathy suddenly focused her gaze on the stage in front of the pews, and Denise said, "Cathy, don't look!"   She knew that Cathy was staring at a ghost, and she didn't want the ghost to start looking back at her. Denise said when they recognize you it gives you the creeps.

Cathy said she saw the ghost of a man standing on the stage as though he was addressing a group. She did not see a group listening to him, however. She had the impression that what he was saying was not good news. The man looked like he belonged in the 1920s. She estimated his height as 5" 11", and said he looked like he was in his 40s or 50s.

Tom had been delayed and he suddenly walked into the church about 20 minutes after Cathy, Denise, and I had first entered the sanctuary. I introduced Tom to Cathy. We didn't tell him anything about what Cathy had said. Denise, Cathy, and I sat in the back pews as Tom went up to the stage. Cathy whispered to us, "I wonder if he will see the ghost of the man. It's on the stage just beside him." Tom then returned and said a man was watching the three of us. I asked him to describe the man and Tom said he was in his 50s. Tom held one of his hands a couple of inches below the top of his head to show how tall the man was. Tom gave his own height as 6" 1" so that would make the man about 5" 11". The three of us were amazed to hear Tom give a description of the ghost that agreed so closely with Cathy's description.

Tom then told Cathy the man asked for her to meet him at the back of the stage. After she had gone up onto the stage, Tom whispered to me that the man wanted her to go down the back hallway to the groom's room where he would give her a spoken message. Tom had not told her this because he wanted to see if she would hear these instructions from the ghost.

Tom also told me that when he had arrived at the church parking lot, he looked up at the window of the groom's room and was shocked to see an image of Kristina, just like the first time he ever came to the church. When he came into the church, he heard the ghost of the man say, "She's here." He wondered if he meant Kristina. Tom said the image of Kristina could have been from his memory, or entities on the other side could also form an image of Kristina if they wanted to. He had no feeling that Kristina was still trapped in the church.

Tom then got up from the pew, and headed toward the groom's room through the south entrance to the back hallway. Cathy was standing by the north entryway to the hallway, and I joined her to see what she had learned. She said the ghost of the man told her to touch the closed door at the entrance of the hallway, and also to touch the closed door of a closet just to its east. When she felt the door of the hallway it felt totally normal, but the door to the closet felt cold and it vibrated like something was trying to get out.

The man wanted her to walk down the hallway, but she didn't want to do it. She had sensed on her previous visit that the ghost in the groom's room was malignant, and said, "This guy's evil." The ghost that had called her to meet him on the stage replied, "Only you can do something about it." I accompanied Cathy down the hallway to the groom's room where we saw Tom sitting in the naugahyde chair. Cathy told Tom what the ghost had told her, and he said, "What does he want you to do about it?" Cathy said, "He didn't tell me." Tom said, "Ask him."

Cathy stepped out into the hallway for a moment, and then I heard her say, "I can't believe it!" Then she told us, "He wants me to call him out and banish him." She also shouted to Denise, who was still out by the pews, that the ghost had said Denise shouldn't come down the hallway, especially from the north end.

Tom asked Cathy if she could cast out the evil spirit immediately. Cathy said she couldn't do it that day because the man told her the evil specter would not listen to her yet. The ghost said, "I will tell you when the time's right." Tom was later to tell me that Cathy is surrounded by darkness that came from persecution she had suffered, and the ghost in the groom's room was surrounded by the darkness of evil. Tom said this made a connection between the two of them that would allow the ghost to be removed through Cathy.

Tom then asked Cathy, "What does a red cross mean to you?" She said she had the feeling it meant, "Pardon me but I need to kill you in the name of God." Tom said that before Cathy had come into the groom's room he had been sitting in the naugahyde chair. He heard a cracking noise in the corner, went over toward where he heard the sound, and saw a red crucifix appear on the top of the left mirror of the cabinet that sits against the wall. He told us that there is definitely a darkness of evil in the room, and the red crucifix can be used to expunge it. He asked Cathy if she was active in helping spirits, and she told him, "I never ignore any requests. When my mom first told me about Kristina, I told her don't you dare turn your back on her."

He also asked Cathy if she had ever worked as a medium. She said, "I never have. I've always been afraid something would grab hold of me and not let me go." When he asked her if she would be willing to serve as a medium to get rid of the evil spirit, she said, "I would have to give it some thought."

As Tom had been sitting in the chair, he watched in the mirror as the groom's room ghost went into the wall behind him. There is a closet on the other side of the wall, and it was the door to this closet that had given Cathy a feeling of cold and vibration when she touched it. Tom asked Cathy why the ghost goes into the wall, and she said he does it to escape people who can see him. She said when people are present who can't see him he just stays in the room. Tom said the ghost does a lot of eavesdropping.

As they talked, Tom and Cathy both noticed a row of footprints showing in the rug of the groom's room. I clearly saw the footprints when they pointed them out to me. They were small and I could plainly see toe prints, showing they must have been made by a barefoot child. I had not closely looked at the rug when I came into the room, but both Tom and Cathy were sure the footprints had not been there when we first entered the room. I made a drawing of the footprints, which turned out so bad it was worthless, and I strongly regretted that none of us had a camera.

Tom then talked about Kristina's ashes, saying that many people think cremation releases a spirit, but it does not. He told about doing some investigations in Palm Springs in the office of a man whose first name was James. Tom was stretched out in the office on a sofa, and there was a black urn hidden in the wall of a secret room behind the sofa. The room was reached by opening a bookshelf that was a secret door, and James had hidden the ashes of his father in the urn that was on the other side of the wall that Tom's head was touching. Tom heard a man's voice say, "Jimmy boy, Jimmy boy, let me out." The man named James turned pale when Tom told him about hearing these words. James had kept his dad's ashes in the box, without telling any other members of his family, and his dad used to call James "Jimmy boy." The shaken man asked Tom to take the ashes and scatter them in the desert.

As Tom continued to talk, he started to ask Cathy various questions to better understand her powers and to see how much instruction she had received in the past to make use of her incredible abilities. Suddenly he asked her if she had problems with her legs. Cathy said she did not. Tom said he sensed energy hovering around her legs. He asked if she experienced anything pulling or tugging at her legs. Cathy said her daughter Carla had hugged her around her legs before she left for the church, and said, "Be careful."

A few days later, I was exchanging messages with Cathy on my computer, and she said she would help remove the evil spirit from the church. She said she would set a date soon. As we talked, I asked her if she heard Tom say he had seen an image of Kristina in the groom's room window after when he first arrived at the church. Cathy said, "Well, I didn't want to say anything because I didn't want to upset my mom, she was already agitated---but you know the little one hugging me?" I asked, "Was that Kristina?" Cathy said it was Kristina in the groom's room and she was hugging Cathy in joyous anticipation of Cathy getting rid of the ghost. She added that Kristina was no longer trapped in the church "but she wants that bad presence evicted and is grateful to the one who can do it."

After we left the church on August 18, 2001, Cathy and Denise followed me home in their car to visit our old family house and orange grove. They were sitting on our sofa talking about what a great place we have to live, when their eyes both instantly focused on a point just behind where my mother was sitting in her rocking chair. They started whispering in each other's ears. My mother said, "You see a ghost don't you?" They said, "Yes." I asked them to describe the ghost, and they said it was a man in his sixties or seventies, with gray hair, and a build that was very solid but not fat. One of them said to the other, "Look, he has a wave in his hair." There was no picture of my father on display anywhere in the house to give them clues about his appearance.

I said, "Let me get a photo album." I got out an album and opened it to a couple of pages where there were many people shown in the photos. My dad was shown a couple of times in photos that included other people along with him. I took the album, laid it in front of them, and asked them if they recognized the spirit. They looked up and down the photos, and then instantly both said, "There he is!" They were pointing at my dad's photo. One said, "See, there is the wave in his hair." Their comment about seeing a wave in his hair amazed me because that was always one of his most favorable features. They said he is extremely fond of my mother, very protective of her, and is happy here. They thought it was a good place for him to be.

This had been one of the most incredible days I have experienced in all of my life. Tom and Cathy had once again shown a stunning ability to independently detect the same ghosts in the church.

Tom had whispered to me that the ghost on the stage wanted Cathy to go down the hallway to the groom's room where that ghost wanted to give her a message, and she got the same instructions and a message from the ghost. We had seen the extraordinary footprints appear on the rug of the groom's room, and then Cathy and Denise had come to my home and seen my dad in spirit form. They had done an extremely convincing job of identifying him. The next day I felt stunned. I had a headache and dizziness, feelings I rarely experience.

Tom told me a couple of specially selected people would be asked to come help Cathy and him remove the man in the groom's room. They would form an energy circle, but it would not be a spirit communication. I would not be part of the circle, but could instead sit nearby taking notes. He explained to me that some extraordinary manifestations might occur during the process, and, if I were part of the circle, I would become distracted, grab for my notebook, and ruin the whole effort.

Tom, Cathy, and I arranged to meet in Mid-September, 2001 to try to get the malevolent ghost out of the groom's room. Tom invited two of the women who work with him to come help assist. Tom, Cathy, and the two other women believed they had sent the groom's room ghost out of the church forever in dramatic fashion, but later Tom sensed his presence again and concluded that the unwelcome ghost had just been hiding and tricked them into thinking he was gone.

In early October 2001, Denise sent me an email asking if we had moved something "rather large" on our place. She said she had an impression that it was dusty, and added that she had picked up an impression that there was something about moving it that my dad didn't like. After I thought a bit, I realized we just had an enormous pile of very dusty, dried, cut-off branches moved away to the dump. These were out of sight of the street behind our buildings, so nobody who had driven by could have seen that the brush pile was gone.

The man who moved the branches proved to be very unreliable. He came and asked for money in advance a couple of times, and never did finish the job. He did not show up when he said he would come, and someone who knew him well told me that he was fairly sure the man is a heroin addict. We also learned that he had not moved our brush to the dump, but dumped it at the home of the man who does our tractor work. He capped his work for our grove man by stealing his generator. During his lifetime, my dad would have been very upset if someone like this had been hired to work on our place.

Denise later told me that she really jumped when she saw my dad in our living room. She used to say that even though she could detect the presence of ghosts in several ways she never really saw them, except for the one time when she and Cathy had simultaneous visions of Denise's son. She never was able to hear them either. Denise had sensed ghosts by feeling their emotions and sometimes she even smelled odors associated with them. She told me she would smell a mint scent when she was near a little girl ghost named Caroline. Later, she said Caroline had left the church. But now Denise had begun to see ghosts in the church. She briefly glimpsed the man on the stage at the same time that Cathy did. A few years ago Denise had been trying with someone's help to get rid of her abilities to sense ghosts, but apparently just the opposite of what she intended took place and her powers were stronger than ever. I wondered if I would become more psychic too if I hung around long enough with Tom, Jan, Denise, Cathy, and the ghosts. I would love to hear what the ghosts have to say, and to see them looking just like living people, dressed in the clothing of their time.

Denise claimed there are so many ghosts in the old church, it resembles a Grand Central Station of the spirit world. She said that since the remaining ghosts don't seem to want help in leaving we will probably just coexist with them from now on. Coincidentally, I have also heard Tom call the church, "Grand Central Spirit Station."

When Denise or Cathy talk about the various ghosts in the church it is usually hard for me to corroborate their observations other than through their agreement with each other and with Tom and Jan. When they came to my home, it stunned me because I could easily identify the spirit they described. I had another chance to marvel at Cathy's accuracy when she went to a ghost investigation that Tom arranged for a group of people at a house in San Bernardino, California.

There were about twenty people at the house who had come to test their ability to sense ghosts. Tom considered several of them to be very sensitive He had not told us any details of the spirit activity that had been observed there. Cathy soon said she saw the ghost of a man in the house, and added that he was very attached to the woman who lived there. Tom then asked Cathy to accompany him to the carport. Cathy stared into the driver's seat of one of the two cars in the carport with a shocked look on her face, and Tom whispered to me, "Ask Cathy what she sees." I did, and she said, "It's the guy from the house."

Tom asked Cathy to describe the man and she said, "He's 5'9" or 5" 10" tall, and he has salt and pepper hair." Tom asked about his build, saying, "Is he fat, or skinny, or what?" Cathy said he was not fat or skinny, didn't have a football player's build either, and she said she would describe him as having a slim build. I asked how old he was and she said he was in his 50s or 60s. Tom replied that Cathy's description was totally accurate, and when she told of seeing the ghost in the driver's seat of one of the two cars parked in the carport, Tom said that the car she had been looking into was the man's car. After everyone finished exploring the house and yard, we gathered in a large room to discuss what each person in the group had observed. But first, Tom asked the woman who owned the house to put a tape in her VCR. We saw a man appear on the TV screen who closely matched Cathy's description. She whispered to me, "That's the guy!" Tom said he had been carefully watching her face when the tape started playing and had seen a look of astonishment when she recognized the man. He had died of cancer a year or two earlier. His widow, who had noticed spirit activity in her house but was skeptical that her husband had come back, was thrilled to tears to see this confirmation of her husband's presence. There was no photo of the woman's husband on display anywhere in the house to help Cathy describe him.

Cathy had been the only one present who saw the ghost and described him. Later, the others in Tom's group gathered around her and raved about her abilities as though she was a rock star. The accuracy that Cathy and her mother had shown in haunted houses gave me even more confidence about their observations in the church.

Cathy and I shared another extraordinary experience while using her oujia board on another occasion. As the two of us placed our hands on the pointer, I barely touched my fingers to it, and made every effort to ensure that I wasn't controlling its direction of movement. Cathy asked, "Does anyone want to communicate?
Answer---Yes
Are you male?
Answer---Yes
What are your initials?
Answer---V.C.
Could you spell your complete name?
Answer---V. Cooles

I was very startled because my grandfather's first name was Vine and his last name was Cooley. I told this to Cathy.
Cathy asked, "Are you related to one of us?"
Answer---Yes
Are you related to John?
Answer---No
Who are you related to?
Answer---Cathy (I assume my grandfather was making a little joke here)
What year were you born?
Answer-1876

This was exactly right.
I asked, "Do you have a message?"
Answer—Ray (my grandfather didn't like the name Vine, often used the initials V.R. Cooley, but most often was called Ray)
Cathy asked, "Are you John's grandfather?"
Answer---Yes
I asked, "Do you have advice for any of our family?"
Answer---Yes
For whom?
Answer---Jean (my mother and his daughter)
What is your advice?
Answer---Sell
Was sell the answer?---Yes

151

Sell our property?---Yes

This is very likely the advice my grandfather would give my mother about the last remaining orange grove in our city. He planted the grove to support his family, which it did during his lifetime, but he probably would not have understood why anyone would want to hold onto it for sentimental reasons during a time when a small farm could no longer support a family. I am certain that Cathy could not have known all the information provided by the ouija board about my grandfather.

It was in 2002 that I finally lost my last traces of skepticism about ghosts. As I mentioned earlier in the book, I had always looked forward to Tom's investigations with an overpowering feeling of excitement because I was always so eager to gather more evidence of the existence of ghosts. When I was waiting for a meeting of Tom and some of his investigators to begin at the old church on May 18, 2002, I realized I no longer experienced excitement. I looked forward to the meeting, but for the first time, no longer with a sense of great urgency for more proof of the existence of ghosts. I felt totally confident that they existed. Since this time I have suffered not one iota of doubt about their existence. It had taken seven years and a vast amount of convincing experience to finally get to this point. I also reached a state of mind where news of someone's death no longer produced the horror in me that it once did, because I knew that they still existed. I can't recall any specific incident that brought an end to my doubts. They finally just seemed to have worn out.

The ghostly events have never stopped in the old church and continue to expand the variety of ghosts and their manifestations. Jan Hagman and Cathy reported seeing the ghost of a man hanging from the ceiling of the church's attic by a rope around his neck.

I received another powerful demonstration from the "other side" in March 2004 after the Death of Kristina's dad, the retired Rialto doctor who bought the old church and adjacent Sunday school building that now serve as the home of the Rialto Historical Society. He was always a strong supporter of the Historical Society, even more so during the last two years of his life when he was dying of cancer. He was a very determined and courageous man. He died on March 1,

152

2004. His memorial service was on Saturday, March 21, 2004 in the old church.

Tom suggested to me before the memorial service that I should walk through the church when it was empty, asking out loud for a demonstration that there is life after death and that Kristina's father still exists. I did this, repeating over and over my request for a sign that there is an afterlife.

After I returned home from the memorial service, I saw that something very strange had happened to the eight clocks in my home. Four of them were exactly on time, near 3 PM, and the other four were exactly one hour slow, near 2 PM. They had been on time when I left for the memorial service, since I kept looking at them to see when I should leave. There had been nobody in the house who had changed the time on the clocks during the time since I had left for the memorial service, and the difference in time can't be explained by an electrical power failure because the clocks are on the same electrical circuits. I had my demonstration.

Other strange things have continued to happen at my house. In February 2008, my brother, Jim, and sister-in-law, Marian, were visiting. Jim, Marian, my mother, and I were all sitting in our kitchen table when a light fixture suddenly went off. I assumed that this had happened when the light burned out from overuse. But when I flicked the switch, it went on again. Some unseen force had turned the switch off as we sat at the kitchen table. I had been facing the switch, so I am certain that nobody had been there to turn it off. Perhaps it was my dad showing my brother and sister-in-law that he still exists.

21 Tom's Ghost Class

In early October of 2001 Tom invited me to attend a class about ghosts he was going to give on a Saturday shortly before Halloween. He said that the class would begin at 10:30 in the morning in a Riverside, California building where he formerly had his vocational rehabilitation business. There would be a break for lunch, to be followed by an afternoon ghost-hunting session in an old cemetery in Riverside. This would be followed by another break for dinner, and then the group would arrive at the old church in Rialto around 7:00 PM, spend time looking for ghosts there, and finish near 9:00. I agreed to let the group in the church at night, but I had several things I needed to do that day, so I said I would not join them for the earlier part of the class. After a little thought, I decided I didn't want to miss anything, especially the visit to the cemetery, so I called Tom and told him I would attend the entire class starting in the morning. I am very glad I did this, because this one-day course was to prove to be the most extraordinary class that I ever attended.

The group that arrived on a sunny, warm day in late October for the ghost class included a gorgeous newspaper reporter named Rachel who has dark brown hair and beautiful brown eyes. Rachel reminded me of the actress Teri Hatcher. Tom had invited her to attend so that she could write a Halloween story about the class for her newspaper. A photographer, named Bill, also came from the newspaper to take photos for Rachel's article. Tom told us that there was a ghost in the building in which we were meeting. It had been encountered by several people, was not too cooperative, and liked to pull a few pranks. He warned Bill that ghosts sometimes sabotage attempts at photography, so Bill should not be surprised if something odd happened when he tried to take pictures.

Of the dozen or so other people who came to take the class, I knew only Mary Barnes and Cathy. Before the class started, Tom asked everyone if they believed in ghosts. Nearly all expressed a conviction that ghosts exist. A couple of people who said they were not certain that there are ghosts, held open the possibility that ghosts may exist, and said they had come to the class in hopes of having that confirmed. Rachel, the reporter, said she believed in an afterlife and in the possibility of prophecies, but she was not sure how many manifestations of spirits were possible because she had never had an experience. Bill, the photographer, said he believed in spirits. That was convenient, because something funny was to happen to some photographs that Bill tried to take that day in the building in Riverside.

Tom began the class by playing a tape recording that he had made at a Redlands, California elementary school. He told us that years ago a boy had rushed into the school parking lot after school looking for his mother who was coming to give him a ride home. He was hit by a car, and carried into the school's office, where he died within a short time. I knew of this tragic accident and had read in a couple of different collections of ghost stories that if you go to the outside of the school building when it is locked and empty, and knock on the window, you will hear the dead boy returning your knocks.

As Tom played the recording you could hear the loud knocks that he and his fellow ghost investigators made, and then faint knocks were heard in reply which became louder as time went on. Tom said these knocks were the ones coming from inside the office, presumably made by the ghost because Tom and the other investigators were certain no living person was inside. As time went on the ghostly knocks became softer until they totally faded out. Tom then turned off the tape recorder.

Bill had been snapping photos of various members of the class with his digital camera before, during, and after the playing of the tape with the knocking sounds. He would periodically check the photos he had taken by looking at the small images with his camera. When he checked his photos a few minutes after the tape had been played, he was astonished to discover that the photos he had taken during the time was tape was playing were all blank. The photos he took before the tape started playing and the photos he took after the tape was turned off had all come out fine. There were a total of nine blank photos. I asked him if he was certain that the nine blank photos were taken during the time the tape was playing, and he said he was. He could remember the photos he took just before and after the tape was played and they had shown up in the camera. Bill recalled that Tom just had told him that prankster ghosts sometimes liked to play tricks on photographers, since it was hard for them to move physical objects but much easier to influence what happened with electronic equipment. He had a spooked look on his face like he thought the correlation between the tape playing and the blank shots was more than coincidence.

How can ghosts sabotage photos? There may be some clues gained by studying psychics who can reportedly use their minds to do the same thing. Dr. William A. Tiller, the same Stanford University physicist mentioned earlier in connection with his theories about dematerialization and materialization of objects, did some experiments that involved a person who appeared to have some mysterious energy that sabotaged his own photography. During the early 1970s, a photographer named Stan came to see Dr. Tiller with a weird tale of 5,000 ruined photographs out of the 9,000 that he had taken during a 15-year period. Strange illuminations showed on the bad photos, and Stan said the same thing happened when he used other people's cameras. Stan blamed his own incompetence for this until he realized that the bad shots correlated with specific "inner states" that he could feel. Stan said that if he snapped a photo when he noticed a particular feeling in both his 7th cervical and 4th thoracic vertebrae the shot was marred with strange optical effects. Stan said he sensed these inner feelings most often at spiritual rock concerts, at religious shrines, and at metaphysical lectures. He sent his camera to Kodak for an evaluation and they reported that it was fine.

Bill Tiller decided to do some experiments in which he mounted the man's sensitized camera and another camera that was not sensitized on a single tripod. Most photo pairs shot with the two cameras showed astounding differences. Photos taken with the sensitized camera showed people as somewhat transparent over parts of their bodies so objects could be clearly seen behind them, whereas photos of the same people taken with the other camera were normal. In addition, when the sensitized camera was fitted with its lens cap, extremely clear photos were shot through this opaque barrier.

Stan could apparently sensitize his camera by merely keeping it close to his body for several days. If he sensitized it and gave it to someone else to use, the photos taken during the next hour by the other photographer would come out badly, but photos taken after that were fine.

How did Bill Tiller explain these incredible results? He concluded that this experiment and other well-controlled studies of a wide range of mind-over-matter type phenomena suggest there are mysterious forms of energy that science can't detect but which can produce strong physical effects under certain conditions. He named these unseen forces "subtle energies" and stated that they are not necessarily weak although they are undetectable by methods now available to science. He believes they may include emotional, mental, and spiritual qualities, as well as other physically intangible factors.

Bill Tiller concluded that there is an unknown type of radiation that can pass through materials that are normally opaque to light, and he speculated that Stan's subtle energy imaged this mysterious radiation via the camera and onto the film. Tiller believed that the camera needed some "energy soaking time" to get charged up by Stan's subtle energy, and this energy would take about an hour to totally leak away unless Stan recharged it by holding it close to his body.

Perhaps ghosts also have "subtle energies" and use them to interfere with photography, including digital cameras as well as older ones that use film, and they may also use the energy fields to move some physical objects. The subtle energies could be what Tom said passed through people's bodies when they held hands in an energy ring, and they might also be the mental energies that Tom asked us to use like laser beams to seal the portal in the church's kitchen during our Halloween ghost investigation. Dr. Tiller believes that subtle energies are involved in remote viewing, precognition, telepathy/mind reading, clairvoyance, clairaudience, psychometry, dowsing, healing, psychokinesis/telekinesis, dematerialization/materialization, levitation, and homeopathy. Rather than explaining the meaning of each of these terms, I will refer readers who are not familiar with them to a dictionary.

Bill, the newspaper photographer, was snapping photos once again when another surprising event happened. Tom had passed out ouija boards for people to use in trying to communicate with the dead.

I had seen ouija boards used often by Tom's group in the old church, and had never seen anything that convinced me that the communications of the group were real. Often, combinations of letters were selected that were nothing more than gibberish, and not words at all.

Mary Barnes had not been at the church during any of Cathy's visits, and Tom's ghost class was the first time they ever met. I knew that both were very ghost-sensitive, and I wanted to see what message they would get if they worked together with a ouija board. They agreed with my request to use a ouija board, and I sat down beside them to record the results. Bill, the photographer, watched them with camera in hand as they took turns asking questions.

Question---Is there a spirit who will be willing to communicate with us?

Answer---Yes

Question---What is your name?

Answer---ALOMOM

Question---Is that your name?

Answer—no answer given

Question---Were you a human?

Answer---Yes

Question---Were you old when you died?

Answer---No

Question---Were you young when you died?

Answer---Yes

Question---How old?

Answer---28

Question---How did you die?

Answer---Suicide

Mary burst into tears. Her son had died of suicide at the age of 28. I had not known this and Cathy had not either. Mary said her son had not been a good speller, and we figured that ALOMOM must mean "hello mom." Mary then began to ask all of the questions.

Question---Are you here for a visit?

Answer---Love

Question---Are you with my mother?

Answer---Yes

Question---Are you at peace?

Answer---Yes, Kiss my kids.

Mary totally broke down in tears, and rushed off. Tom took her into his office to comfort her.

Bill and I were both totally astounded. Bill excitedly called Rachel over to tell her what had happened. Bill's photo of Mary and Cathy using the ouija board later appeared in the newspaper with the caption, "woman getting message from her dead son."

By mid-afternoon, Tom said it was time to go to the cemetery. He had talked to us for several hours about many aspects of ghosts, assigned us some exercises in class to try out various techniques for detecting ghosts, and now we were going to see if we could put our new knowledge to use in the cemetery. Tom said it is often wrongly claimed that cemeteries are free of ghosts. He told us that ghosts go to cemeteries because they know their relatives visit there. He said he would have preferred for us to go to the old church in the afternoon, since ghosts can be found there anytime, followed by a visit to the cemetery at night. But vandals or devil worshippers sometimes enter the cemetery at night, and he feared that police would show up and spoil our experiment. He told us that if they appeared during the day, we should say we were just there to do genealogy and they would not bother us.

The Riverside cemetery had some sections that were green and neat, but a large section was shockingly run-down, with tipped-over grave markers and large areas of bare soil where grass had been allowed to die. I walked with Cathy into the unkempt part of the cemetery, and asked her if she saw any ghosts. She said she could see about a dozen. She said they were of varying ages, some had old-fashioned clothes of the 1800s, and none of them looked haggard. I didn't see any ghosts.

Cathy pointed toward a prematurely white-haired man named Mel from Tom's class who was quite a distance from us, and told me that a ghost was teasing him. She told me that ghosts sometimes want people to know they are there, but they don't want to fully divulge themselves. After a moment, she said the ghost had left him. Later, at dinner, Cathy talked to Mel, and he said he had felt negative energy (meaning bad feelings that he connected with a ghost) in the cemetery for a period of time. She said his statements confirmed what she had told me in the cemetery.

Cathy said that a ghost in an old-fashioned dress was standing very near to us in the cemetery and watching us, and sure enough, when I held my pendulum as motionless as I possibly could, it began to swing in a counterclockwise direction. We then walked to a better-maintained part of the cemetery where Tom and several others in his class had gathered by a grave. He said he had been walking along with a woman named Connie Brooks when she told him the name "Isabel" suddenly popped into her head. They both looked down at a memorial stone they had been approaching, and it read, "Isabel E. Hillanger Concert Pianist Mar 2, 1886---May 22, 1976."

Tom had been placing a tape recorder by certain of the memorial stones after asking spirits to give a message. Before he placed the tape recorder on Isabel's grave, we heard him speaking into the tape recorder to give information about the time of day and the cemetery marker information so that he could identify this specific segment for future reference if anything of interest would show up on it. We were very near a city street that ran through the middle of the cemetery, and cars were whizzing by at high speed.

Tom placed the tape recorder on the grave, and let it run for several minutes. Then he began to search for the place on the tape where it had started recording. We heard segments recorded at other graves before he reached Isabel's marker, and then heard his voice on the tape introducing the most recent piece of recording and the sound of a couple of cars speeding past. After the tape had been playing for a short time, we were astounded to clearly hear faint sounds that resembled piano keys being struck. We had heard nothing like these sounds when the tape was being recorded. Tom played the tape several times as the class, including the newspaper reporter and photographer, gathered around to listen. The Halloween newspaper article included a photo listing our names and showing us listening to the tape. It was captioned, "Group listening to piano music in the cemetery." I figured that a lot of people would really think we were crazy after they read that.

When the class had dinner that evening before concluding the day with a visit to the old church, Tom played the tape recording again so we could hear the piano sounds once more. We were all dumbfounded to learn that now the segment of tape with the piano sounds was totally missing. The recordings made just before and after it were still on the tape, but the one made at Isabel's grave was gone, and there wasn't even a stretch of blank tape to mark its former location.

Hardcore skeptics might assume that Tom had concocted an elaborate trick to fool the newspaper people and the rest of us. Did he visit the cemetery earlier, and find the grave with the inscription "concert pianist?" I don't think he could have recorded the entire segment earlier because his remarks and the traffic sounds on the tape matched so exactly what we had heard a moment before as the tape was recording. Before going to the cemetery, could he have doctored a tape so that it had piano-like sounds on it, allowing him to record his remarks and the traffic noises in the cemetery in the precise location just before the already existing piano sounds on the tape? Finally, could he have rushed into the restaurant's restroom or some other place out of the view of the class just before dinner to totally remove the segment of tape with the piano sounds? Remember there wasn't even a stretch of blank tape left between the preceding and following graveside recordings so it would not have been enough to merely erase that part of the tape. I can't prove that he did not do these things, but I find it highly doubtful he could accomplish such elaborate trickery after having observed the difficulty he has in even using his own computer and other electronic equipment. Also, I don't believe he is a good enough actor to register the tremendous astonishment he showed.

After dinner, we went to the church to finish the all-day ghost class. Most in the class had never been there before. After a short talk from Tom, they began to prowl around looking for ghosts. Tom was anxious to see if anyone would be able to sense the location of the ghost portal in the church kitchen that he had first pointed out to us on the Halloween night of 1997. As described previously, Cathy, during her first visit to the church in July 2001, had sensed the presence of ghost portals that allowed ghosts to come and go. She had said that she felt like she would be sucked into the portals. She described a ghost portal in the church kitchen in the exact same location where Tom had said it was, although she had never been in the church before. She described it as about two feet wide, taller than it was wide, and having jagged edges which glowed like an aura.

Now, Tom told Connie Brooks, who had never been in the church before and who, he said, had never been told about the portal, to walk through the south entrance to the kitchen with her eyes closed. He watched silently as she headed straight for the spot where he had said there was a portal. She said, "There is a very interesting energy here that makes me swirl. It is a vertical energy." I imagine she said this because she felt like she was going to be sucked upward. Tom was beaming. Connie was standing in the exact spot where he had claimed there was a portal. A man dressed all in black named John Blankenship took photos throughout the church, and was startled to notice that one aimed into the south entrance of the kitchen contained a strange, transparent shape in the same spot where people had stated there is a portal.

Most people in the class claimed to have encounters with ghosts that evening. Mary Barnes told of seeing her pendulum begin to swing wildly with very wide arcs, and then come to an abrupt stop in mid air. She saw this happen several times. Other people told of seeing ghosts, or of being pushed, pulled, or even tripped by them.

Rachel, the newspaper reporter, said she was coming down the stairs holding firmly onto the railing when she felt her foot bump against something and she fell. Strangely, there was nothing for her foot to catch against in that location. Tom said he felt like he had been pushed when he was coming down the stairs. He said that poltergeist-like spirits often push people or knock them down.

Rachel said she had a very eerie feeling in several places. In the downstairs storeroom that has given Tom and Denise such bad feelings she said she felt a negative, sinister energy, and smelled a strange sour odor. She said it gave her a creepy feeling and she didn't stay long. She told us she had a weird feeling in the hallway by the groom's room, saw light violet spots in the darkened bride's room, and saw faces in the stained glass windows in addition to those painted there.

Bill, the newspaper photographer, was surprised to hear his ex-wife's voice on his cell phone when he was in the sanctuary, because he believed she did not know his number. He also felt someone constantly tugging at the pager on his belt, although no one was there. He smelled a strong pungent odor by a long unlit candle, and said he felt "serious tingling" in his legs. Also he was very startled when he checked the photos from his digital camera and saw that the ones he made in the sanctuary contained many brightly-colored little balls of light---a phenomena sometimes reported in photos made in haunted buildings. Bill was clearly amazed by his experiences. As mentioned earlier, orbs have also showed up in photographs taken by other people in the church, including some that I took.

I had predicted to the people sitting next to me at dinner before we went to the church that when the newspaper article came out it would tell of our experiences, but not those of the newspaper reporter and photographer. That is exactly what happened when the story appeared in the newspaper on Halloween.

22   What Does it all Mean?

I have described to you a large number of incidents that involved meetings between people and ghosts. Most of them were taken from detailed notes I kept over a period of some eight years. My intention was to allow you to accompany me on a journey that has literally shattered my belief system. I feel somewhat like I would have had I met Disney's Donald Duck and learned that he was real. The bad news, of course, is that a belief in ghosts is somewhat more awkward in our society than a belief in soil science. The good news is that my belief system was probably due for some opening up.

A belief in a spirit world has undermined my feelings of certainty about cause and effect relationships. I had always assumed that whatever happened in the world had a natural cause, but after my experiences with ghosts I am no longer sure of that. If something seems to vanish mysteriously or if I find it in a totally unexpected place, I am no longer certain that I just forgot where I put it, and wonder if a spirit could have done it. Could an evil spirit be responsible for a tragedy shown on the evening news, or could a beneficent one be behind an amazing narrow escape? I look at the world now as spirit filled, often viewing things more like an ancient person than a modern one. I used to think that eventually science will find explanations for most phenomena of interest to humans. But if ghosts exist and are capable of such acts as appearing, disappearing, and communicating with us, science is going to have to broaden its scope.

The thought of a supernatural world is anathema to western science. If the supernatural and natural are ever reconciled, it will not occur for a long time. It is not uncommon for scientists, especially mature ones, to be members of an organized religion, but they usually tend to keep science and faith separated in their minds. Some make the effort to interweave the two, but they are few and their efforts have in general not influenced the allergy most scientists show for the mystic. In fact, "mystic" and "supernatural" are in a way definitions for things that scientists cannot explain, and scientists are not fond of such things unless they have a strategy to try to figure them out. As an example, present scientific methods neither prove nor disprove the existence of souls. Even if they could be detected, if they are immortal they must be impervious to all effects of familiar matter and energy. A soul or ghost standing beside an exploding nuclear weapon would supposedly be unharmed. This "soul stuff" would not resemble any material familiar to science, nor act consistently with presently accepted "natural" laws. But although we are still all believers in science, we are realizing that science may never be able to answer larger questions about human existence. Social explorations such as the New Age movement, alternate medicine, diet fads, and the various cults so vilified in the media are signs that people are looking elsewhere.

It is likely that belief in ghosts will increase as the fear of ridicule for telling ghost stories decreases and more people hear about ghosts from those they trust. I believe that this is already happening because so many people I talk to seem to believe in ghosts or at least in the possibility of them. When I give talks about ghosts to groups of people, I notice that most of them seem intensely interested, and only a few appear incredulous. In fact, the subject of ghosts draws vastly more interest than any other topic I have ever discussed. Of course, I am taking the risk by espousing their existence rather than the people in my audiences.

Coming to believe in ghosts has also led to some disillusionment about things I had formerly admired almost limitlessly---science and universities. The mocking of any belief in ghosts by so many of these learned people now makes them seem foolishly closed minded considering the countless reports of ghosts that have appeared throughout history. I can't blame the skeptics too harshly, since I had the same outlook myself. I have wondered if I could have come to the conclusion that there is a spirit world without having the direct experiences that I did, and I feel certain that I could not have. I feel extremely fortunate to have had these experiences and obviously encourage others to be more open to them. If anyone wants similar ones, I believe they can probably have convincing encounters with ghosts if they are willing to spend years in our old church. This would be welcome since we never have enough volunteer workers.

My experiences with ghosts have also obviously caused me to think more deeply about religion. I have become less of an agnostic about religion and more of a questioner of science.

It is difficult to see how ghosts or souls would have evolved by natural selection during an evolutionary process. Is a creator involved? In the past I have dismissed the thought of an overwhelming intelligence as something invented because of the seductive appeal of an afterlife. I am not a creationist in that I don't believe the biblical story of Genesis literally. But now I no longer dismiss the idea of a larger power. Finding good evidence to determine the nature of a creator and the supernatural side of existence has always seemed impossible to me. However, the world certainly seems to be rich with revelations. Julia, the English singer whose terrifying visit to the church is related in Chapter 13, asked not long after her visit to the church to see a divine sign to show her if Christianity is the true religion. She had a crucifix that was lying flat on a table, and she was astounded when she entered the room after making her request for a sign and saw that the crucifix was balanced on its side. She again placed the crucifix flat on the table, and was later dumbfounded a second time when she saw that the crucifix was once again balanced on its side. She was certain that no living mortal had raised the crucifix and balanced it on its side, and she asked my nephew Bob how he thought this could be interpreted. Bob suggested that they go to see a Catholic Priest. When Julia described what had happened, the priest said that there are many miracles, and this was her miracle. She was extremely impressed, and I was too when she told me about it, although I was not totally convinced. I was not as certain as she was that nobody could have tilted it on edge.

If there is a higher power, or a single god, does one religion have a better description of it, her, or him. All people who choose a religion seem to be sure that theirs is the "right" one. Some are flexible, such as Hinduism that allows you to be both a Hindu and a member of another religion. But many of them, such as Islam and Christianity, consider worship of any other god to be blasphemy. We are all aware of how, in warfare, God seems to be on the side of all parties. Spirits exist in most religions, whether they are monotheistic or polytheistic. I asked Cathy and Denise, since they were involved so deeply in the search for the ghosts in the church, whether the supernatural world implied the existence of an all-powerful God, or whether it could be the type of a world described by prophets such as Buddha. They both believed a God/creator was necessary.

When I asked Cathy how she was sure there was one God instead of several Gods, she replied that it was difficult to be certain, but that if there were several gods rather than one supreme being there would be conflicts among them. Just for curiosity, I asked her what she thought happened to atheistic or agnostic skeptics, wondering if she would think they would be sent to burn forever in a blazing Hell. She laughed and said she thought they would just get their butts kicked for awhile, and then they would be all right. In her mind it didn't make sense to blame them for being unbelievers because they had not been fortunate enough to see evidence that would show them that there was a supernatural world. Denise agreed with this, and said people shouldn't be blamed for not knowing there was a spiritual existence, but they would suffer blame for doing things that they knew were wrong. This made sense to me, of course, not only because I have spent the vast majority of my life being an agnostic, but also because some of the best people I have ever known---the kindest and most considerate of others, most self-sacrificing, with the highest moral standards, and noblest in all their actions--- have been atheists or agnostics. It is commendable to be such a person, I believe, because they are not behaving admirably just because of the promise of eternal reward or the fear or eternal punishment but simply because they think it is the right thing to do. Some of the worst people I have ever known have also been atheists.

I have not been newly born by my experience with ghosts, but I must admit I am becoming more interested in religion. Obviously I find the concept of an afterlife both appealing and comforting. In the past, when people died I thought they were gone forever. Now that I no longer believe this, the world seems a less brutal place. Obviously this is one of the compelling advantages for belief. Since I spent most of my life in environments where the majority were Christians (although usually non-practicing) I am learning more about

Christianity. I am reading up on the teaching of Jesus and am taken with the Sermon on the Mount. Who knows, my ghost experiences might even make a churchgoer out of me. In that case, everyone will merely think that I imagined all of these ghost incidents and wrote this book because I was becoming older and more frightened of death. For the information of you readers, it is true that I am becoming older and am not happy with the idea of death, but I definitely did not imagine these ghost incidents!

My personal discovery that ghosts are real seems in some ways to have added more confusion than clarity to my thinking. The idea that when you die your consciousness is extinguished forever couldn't be simpler or clearer. My conclusion that there is an afterlife filled with uncertainties brings a feeling of confusion that will probably last until I get there.

As I said in the introduction, if you are a believer in ghosts, hopefully this book will strengthen your belief. If you are unsure, open yourself to experiences and find your own Tom. If you are a doubter, the book probably did not convince you that they exist, but maybe you should also look a little harder. If you think I am nuts, join the throng. I am sure I am opening myself to ridicule by writing this book, but I am no stranger to such treatment. I used to write environmental impact statements about controversial topics such as the use of the desert by off-road vehicles when I worked for the Bureau of Land Management. My research showed that off-road vehicles did more damage than the off-road vehicle community wanted to believe, but less than the environmental movement expected. My work therefore weakened both of their political positions and resulted in an amazing flood of extremely insulting letters. I had become a villain to both camps. The topic of ghosts cannot compete in vehemence. In fact, if this book suffers no attacks it will mean that it has not reached the number of readers that I had hoped. Controversy engenders thinking. May the ghosts be with you.

Made in the USA